Darkness in the Clouds

The Art of Spiritual Warfare and Demonic
Oppression

Terrence Covin

Truth & Praxis

Darkness in the Clouds

Unless otherwise specified, all Scripture quotations from the Holy Bible, English Standard Version. ESV® Text Edition: 2016. Copyright © 2001 by Crossway Bibles, a publishing ministry of Good News Publishers. -

Paperback ISBN: 979-8-9872665-1-9

eBook ISBN: 979-8-9872665-0-2

Typeset by Terrence Covin

Cover design by Terrence Covin

Printed in the United States of America

Contents

Preface

Welcome and thank you for taking a leap of faith into this book with me. I struggled with how best to present this information to audiences who are already Christians, and to those who may not be. But to be honest, I simply couldn't write this book in a way that is stripped from the much-needed Christian foundation it rests upon. My own personal journey in life would not allow it. For to remove this foundation would be to give you a book that attempts to extinguish God's glory, leaving a book that could be misconstrued as nothing more than musings of one's own imagination. It would not be authentic or God-honoring. As you experience this book, it will be presented as if you are a Christian. However, even if you're not, the information will still be immensely valuable to your own human existence. In fact, I'd argue that if you're not a Christian, the information presented to you is even more necessary and critical than if you already were.

Introduction

THIS IS A STORY I've been wanting to tell for over a decade. And while it's been at the forefront of my mind for the last ten years, it has been pressing against my soul since I was a child. However, I'd like to warn you: This book isn't for the faint of heart. What you're going to read will challenge you on many fronts. It will challenge the way you perceive life. It will challenge what you've come to know as your identity as part of God's creation. It will also challenge your faith and what you've come to believe about His creation. I hope that by the end of this book you will be able to see the world for what it truly is, while growing in an understanding of the supernatural forces at work. I repeat, this will be a challenge, but, I believe, a much needed one in our day and age.

I often wonder how many of us are truly challenged in our walk with God, and do we test what we know about life. How often do you challenge your own beliefs? I'd argue that most of the challenges we endure center around things that are corporeal and self-focused. For example, as Christians we tend to concentrate on issues relating to our health, marriage, death, finances, relocations, transitions, and areas of habitual sin. All of these concerns can shape what we believe about God. And they can and often do challenge our faith in Him. It is in these times that we may, as the psalmist did, call out for the Lord to strengthen our resolve in Him:

God is our refuge and strength, a very present help in trouble. Therefore we will not fear though the earth gives way, though the mountains be moved into the heart of the sea, though its waters roar and foam, though the mountains tremble at its swelling. Selah (Psalm 46:1–3, ESV)

In our prayers we tend to seek encouragement, strength, hope, and relief from the strain and stresses of life. We desire God to be our refuge and our shelter. He is the rock upon which we lean. We desire to come out of the opposite end of our struggles with a stronger, more resilient faith. Challenged, but victorious! Sometimes we do and sometimes we don't. But the reality is we often appeal to God through what we see and what we desire to see. And what we desire to see is usually based on what we know about life. This can create a vicious cycle. What tends to happen is we ask God to challenge our faith or come to our rescue, but only in a way that doesn't make us uncomfortable. Or we may ask in a way that only aligns with what we've already come to believe about His creation and how it operates. It is a truly limiting affair.

Speaking of limitations, one of the reasons many believers struggle so much with their faith is because they can become too shortsighted and trapped within their traditional church frameworks. These frameworks are built on comfort and theological doctrines that have been handed down for millennia. Don't be fooled. Everyone has an operational framework, even atheists. These frameworks consist of the ideas, doctrines, and beliefs we all use to operate in the world, which shape our own identity. Oftentimes they are packed with ideas that we should question but never do, simply for the sake of keeping the framework intact. For if we dare to rattle the cage who knows what we might shake loose.

But this shortsightedness leaves us ill-equipped for the real world and breeds issues that are counterproductive to our walk of faith. Church tradition ends up supplanting truth and the issues of the world end up taking precedence over the concerns of the kingdom. This leaves salvation as just a badge of honor but not a call to arms. And why would it be? Who would we be fighting against? After all, Jesus defeated death and Satan on the cross. With His last words He declared, "It is finished" (John 19:30). All that is left are corrupt humans and a fallen world, right? Sure, we know Satan is kicking rocks here and there and disturbing the peace, but what is he *really* doing that we should care? We may talk of the devil who "prowls around like a roaring lion, seeking someone to devour" (1 Peter 5:8) and proclaim we need to "put on the whole armor of God" (Ephesians 6:11), but then we struggle to find practical ways to really integrate these ideas into our daily lives.

One of my pastors describes the way we regurgitate Scripture and doctrine at times as nothing more than "Christianese." Our Christian language can sound good and be generally accurate, but it doesn't usually have any real impact on the world. Does putting on the armor of God apply when someone cuts us off while driving down the highway? Is Satan trying to get the best of us while we're heading to work at a job we probably don't even like? Are Satan and his army operating in dark alleys, strip clubs, or poverty-stricken neighborhoods? Is it the work of the devil when the person we voted for does not get elected? Are these the demonic forces at work we should be fighting against?

Put another way, are we really just contending against sinful people—including ourselves—or real demonic beings? While many Christians may proclaim they're fighting against the enemies of darkness, how many of us have actually dealt with real demonic forces—the kind that plagued the early world, the ancient days of Israel, Jesus, the disciples, or the Apostle Paul? How many of us are really just speaking Christianese?

God isn't constrained by our shortsightedness. His abilities aren't limited by our knowledge of what makes up reality or our understanding. Put another way, God is in the heavens, and He does whatever He pleases (see Psalm 115:3). I've come to learn there are things in this world that exist whether we desire to believe in them or not. God's creation is not constrained by our belief systems. His creation is not predicated on what we deem to be true or false. He is the Potter; we are the clay.

At a young age I became aware of my own limited reasoning when I started encountering demonic activity. All that I had come to know about life seemed to change in an instant. And I soon realized that I didn't know much at all.

I hope you will take away from this book this truth: *that the world with all its brokenness is not the complete picture of our world.* We would do better to press past what we can see and to petition God for sight that goes beyond the flesh. Only then can we come to fully understand the world we live in, our God, and what is at stake.

His Will Not Mine

For as far back as I can remember, I had the misfortune of experiencing things that today as a believer I know were demonic. As a child I just knew them to be pure, unadulterated evil experiences. What made these instances of horror so much more troubling for me was the initial difficulty in discerning how much was imagination and how much was real. Like most children, I was no foreigner to the "monster in the closet," night terror escapades that most parents and doctors dismiss as an overactive imagination. I was simply a victim of too much Halloween candy, regular church attendance, or a scary television show.

These experiences have always stuck with me. Before I grew up I was convinced they were real, so much so that I didn't view God as a loving Father but more as an angry deity who does whatever He pleases. I concluded that He found pleasure in cursing me for no good reason. Thankfully, God saved me from my own ignorance and my own shortsighted view of Him and the world He created. But that transformation came at a cost. While God freed my soul, He opened my eyes so I could now see behind the veil of what we call reality. I did not request to see behind the veil, God placed this burden on me without ever asking for my permission. Isn't this just like God? *Hello, Job...we need to talk.*

The burden of carrying experiences that are demonic is heavy. It isn't something most people are faced with. The church in America, while willing to acknowledge the existence of supernatural evil, isn't really filled with many believers who've actually had encounters with it. On the other hand, there are those who claim everything is of demonic oppression and would attempt to cast water out of a cup to prove it. The unfortunate result of this is silence on the matter. Who wants to be seen as the crazy one in the bunch? *Sure, everyone believes in evil forces and Satan. The Bible says they exist, right?* Isn't that what *all* Christians claim they believe? Because I didn't want to seem like a crazed bat, I rarely ever disclosed my own experiences as a child. In fact, growing up I would often find more comfort in confiding my stories to nonbelievers than believers. By and large, those whom I knew as Christians claimed to believe in evil, supernatural forces, but it was always the nonbelievers I knew who were truly interested in the details. It was akin to the difference of believing Jesus *is* God versus believing *in* Jesus *as* God. I often wondered if Christians actually experienced demonic activity at all. Or were they just hiding their stories, tucking them away to save face amongst their brethren?

The experiences I've faced have placed me on a spiritual island. However, I'm firmly convinced I am not the only one on this island. I believe there are others—Christians or not—who are simply too scared to voice their story. And living as an islander has cultivated in me a certain state of mind. One that would not allow me to reconcile certain truths with what I was taught concerning the Christian faith. The inability to reconcile the faith I was taught and what I'd experienced created great tension within my entire being. And that tension constantly challenged what I knew about creation and our God.

I often asked myself why it was necessary for demons to exist. Why would God allow Satan to roam the earth? Why was Satan in the garden to begin with? Why do demons, who are supposed to be fallen angels, hate humans? What did humans ever do to them? Why did *I* have to experience demonic activity? Where was my loving God during my childhood? And, more pressing and weighty to my soul, why couldn't the Church deliver any satisfactory answers that go beyond the template of tradition? In fact, the church, the one place that should fully understand this reality, is typically inept at even diagnosing when spiritual activity is present. We no longer know how to look for clues, so to cover our bases we often shrug our shoulders and just appeal to ignorance, comforting ourselves with the thought that nobody knows but God. While this certainly may be the case in many instances, we've become too quick to throw the baby out with the bath water. It's easier to acquiesce and appeal to ignorance than to challenge ourselves to search for answers. Again, who wants to seem crazy in the midst of Christian intellectuals? Besides, there are real issues to deal with like poverty, injustice, divorce, and habitual sin. Who wants to talk about something nobody can see let alone really understand?

But it is an odd thing. Those who came before us weren't concerned with what others thought when faced with certain truths. The Bible starts off with spiritual activity when God appears and speaks creation into existence. Soon after the creation event the serpent initiates a conversation that leads to the fall. The Old

Testament is filled with demonic activity, such as the Canaanite practice of worshipping Baal (see Judges 2:11, Deuteronomy 4:3), Saul seeking mediums (see 1 Samuel 28:7) and Job being tempted (see Job 1:6). This narrative continues as Jesus leads the charge against the demonic spiritual forces that are ravaging humanity like hounds of hell feasting on fresh flesh (see Mark 1:39). During Jesus' time on earth His disciples bore witness to this same activity (see Matthew 17:19). The apostle Paul also wrote about the demonic activity he faced (see 2 Corinthians 12:7).

And let us not forget the early Church fathers such as Justin Martyr, Tertullian, Athanasius, and Origen, who likewise wrote about the existence of demonic activity in their day. Tertullian, in his book *Apology*, went so far as to help the Romans understand that their gods—while not gods in the Christian sense—were spiritual beings that were actually demonic:

So this divinity of yours is no divinity; for if it were, it would not be pretended to by demons, and it would not be denied by gods. But since on both sides there is a concurrent acknowledgment that they are not gods, gather from this that there is but a single race —I mean the race of demons, the real race in both cases. Let your search, then, now be after gods; for those whom you had imagined to be so you find to be spirits of evil. (Tertullian, Apology, Ch. 23)

What we see throughout the history of our faith is a consistent narrative that has been woven into the very fabric of human existence: *That evil spiritual forces are real*. Yet in our modern day and age, this narrative that was once at the forefront of some of the greatest minds of the faith has somehow taken a back seat.

I hope this book will cause you to shake off the chains of tradition, to look more closely at what God has revealed about creation, and to place the narrative concerning demonic activity back into the Christian conversation. Ultimately this should free you to see the world in a new way, the way God intended you to see it, helping you to recognize that: salvation in Christ is more than just a badge of honor; that your life is exponentially more valuable than you may have imagined; that your purpose is spiritual, not earthly; that you are part of the greatest story that could be conceived of by the greatest mind and that it is still being written; and finally, that you will seek new challenges that go beyond what you could have imagined, so that the impacts of your life are *eternally* realized within the kingdom. All while bringing God glory.

So, let's begin, shall we?

—Terrence Covin

Chapter One

Thunder of God

I COULDN'T HAVE BEEN more than five years old. I had just finished watching an episode from the *Land of the Lost*, a children's sci-fi adventure television series created in the '70s. Back then the special effects were riveting and certainly terrifying enough to captivate the mind of such a young naïve boy. To be honest I'm not sure what sucked me into this show. Perhaps it was the jittery and creepy movements from the stop-motion dinosaur figures. Or the idea of innocently rafting down a river only to end up in another world. Maybe it was Chaka, the hairy childlike ape figure with the epic forehead. Or possibly it was the banjo, which was the backdrop instrument during the introduction to each episode. Yes, a banjo.

This evening my mom was at work, and it was just my dad and me. At least that's how I remember that day. See, I grew up in a military household. Both my parents served in the United States Air Force. Those of us who grow up this way are often referred to as military brats. It was quite common for one of my parents to be deployed or on tour or working late because the grown-ups were "playing war" in what they called "exercises." So tonight's crew consisted of only my towering dad and me.

That night, as the show—chock-full of backyard terrain camera shots, poor green screening, and plastic dinosaurs—came to an end, my father signaled it was time for me to go to bed. I remember not wanting to go just yet. I mustered up any fuel reserves I had left in my five-year-old tank to show I wasn't tired. My dad decided to use another tactic, which was to scare me into going to bed. He proceeded to tell me that monsters would come and get me if I didn't go to bed. Now, obviously I wasn't in my right mind and my tiredness was showing because I believed him. I mean, let's just think about this rationally for a second. The monsters are supposed to come visit you when you are *in* the bed, not while you're *out* of the bed. I did mention that I was naïve, didn't I?

Begrudgingly I made my way down the hall to my bedroom. At the time we were staying in what was called billeting, essentially a military hotel. This is normally where military families stay while transitioning from one military base to another. The living quarters were often pretty small, which meant the bedrooms were tiny and minimalistic. My room had a bed, a dresser with a lamp, and a dark brown, free-standing metal closet. I remember the closet sounding like the thunder of God whenever I opened or closed it.

After getting ready for bed, teeth now polished and pajamas suited up, it was time for the customary good-night prayer. This moment in time is the earliest memory I have of anything relating to Christianity. And what was so striking about this event is that my dad practically *never* went to church during my childhood. Yet, he came from a family of churchgoers. On the other hand, my mom doesn't come from a family of churchgoers, but she religiously toted my younger sister and me to church each week. And I'm not going to lie, I hated it. Life has an odd way of working itself out.

That night my dad took the lead and I followed. Praying at bedtime became something of a habit for me as I grew up, and if I had to pinpoint when the habit started, it would be this day. I'm sure I was praying before then, but the reason this day sticks out to me so much is because of what happened next.

I watched my dad leave my bedroom after wishing me a good night. I remember lying there for a few minutes looking up at the ceiling, just waiting for the feeling of sleep to finally hit me. That evening it was taking a bit longer than I expected. I turned over onto my stomach to relax. That's when I heard it: The thunder of God. My closet started making a noise. I could hear the metal flexing in and out like something was moving around inside it. Something was in my closet trying to make its way out. I could hear the closet buckling under the weight of whatever it was. I froze. To this day I don't even remember breathing for the next two minutes. The door slid open and then I heard nothing. Absolute silence. But not just your normal silence, it was akin to being trapped inside a vacuum that had sucked any semblance of noise out of the room. I lay there with my eyes closed, too terrified to move. While I could hear nothing, I could feel everything. I could feel whatever it was moving closer to me, almost like energy. It felt wrong. Horribly wrong. As I felt this presence moving closer, I realized my left hand was hanging off the bed. Crap! I was too afraid to move it, still believing if I stayed still long enough this presence wouldn't notice me. That plan backfired because, before I knew it, something grabbed my hand slowly, almost meticulously. After this presence let go, I could feel it moving back toward the closet. More sounds of thunder as it made its way into the huge box of metal standing against my wall. The closet door closed. I lay there, still not moving and still not breathing. I lay there for a long time, feeling my heart beat through my chest and throat. I had never experienced anything like that before.

Days later I tried to rationalize what had happened. Yes, even at an early age. I asked my dad if he was the *monster* in my room that night, thinking surely he managed to slip under my bedroom door without me knowing it. After all, he was the one that gave me the tip about monsters in my bedroom, so it all seemed too convenient. Of course, he said no, but that was to be expected. Any good pranksters would never reveal their tricks. I chalked it up to some freak occurrence and an overactive imagination with my dad pulling off an amazing scare tactic. Even to this day I'm still not totally convinced it wasn't him. Maybe I fell asleep and didn't realize it. Perhaps he snuck in when I turned over onto my stomach. Maybe I watched too much big-headed Chaka that night. Is it possible I *thought* I saw him leave when he didn't? Sure, I guess anything is possible, right? Skepticism, save me.

Death of Possibilities

As a child nothing seems impossible. The level of ignorance we all possess coming into this world is astounding. Sure, it's expected. But it's still astounding. I often tell my kids that life isn't what you think it is. As a parent I'm often struck with guilt as I crush their utopian dreams of how the world really works. No, life is not a Disney movie. The faces each of them made when they found out cartoons weren't real was tantamount to me stealing their "wooden idol" at gunpoint. Trying to explain to them the concept of death when my wife's grandmother passed away was like teaching a three-year-old geometry using sign language. The idea that a human could simply disappear was hard for them to grasp.

But that's just it. Many of us are born into this amazing creation believing we can do anything or become anyone. No limits. As an adult I love dreaming that I'm flying, and I'm pretty ticked when I wake up before hitting full speed. Seriously. What the heck, yo? I mean, can I be real for a second?

You're in this dream. One of your favorites! And you start to realize you're dreaming. You're really about to do something incredible so you lean into the dream a bit more, knowing you're free. This is going to be great! This dream will go down in history! The world is your oyster! And then, before you make another move ... you're awake! Nooooo!

Who designed this surreal labyrinth of mockery we call life? Can't a man even dream in this world? The answer to the riddle is a resounding *no*. Utopia in any sense isn't obtainable, even in dreams. And as we grow up we learn possibilities aren't really endless. We replace fiction with facts to the point that we lose most of our God-given creativity. Our new hope is that life can become closer to utopia if we leave behind our childlike ways of thinking and apply more knowledge, facts, and science—you know, grown-up stuff. We no longer compete against each other with creativity. Instead, we compete against each other with our education and intellectual prowess. We're no longer open to ideas or concepts that we can't see let alone explain. In our pursuit for knowledge, we forget we are the creation, not the Creator.

Adulthood is where possibilities go to die. The death of our creative childhood ushers in the impossibility of us grasping the full realities of life. Instead, what we know as life becomes contained in a box that we can easily manage. This helps us cope with everything around us and gives us some semblance of control. However, the odd thing about life is the more we attempt to control it, the less we are in control. The more we attempt to shape and mold God's creation, the more it kicks back and reminds us that we are the clay in the hands of an infinite Potter.

Chapter Two

Where It All Started

IT WAS THE FALL of 1983, and I was seven years old. My parents had received orders for our family to move to Plattsburgh Air Force Base, located in Plattsburgh, New York. We had the pleasure of staying in billeting again while we waited for base housing to open up. We arrived late in the evening, and my mother was working diligently to get my sister and me settled in and ready for bed.

While getting acclimated I heard this incredible roaring sound for a moment and then it would die down. Again, it would roar up and die down. When the roaring geared up it sounded like the whole world was coming to an end, followed by a huge *oh never mind* as the noise died down. Never in my life had I heard such an obnoxious sound. It went on roaring up and dying down all night. I later learned the noises were aircraft engines. My parents had been deployed to the 380th Air Refueling Squadron. The base was the home of KC-135 aircraft, and my dad was an aircraft mechanic. Over the upcoming months and following years the roaring was something I grew accustomed to. It became a normal part of life on the base. So normal that when I didn't hear the constant roaring

I wondered if something was wrong, like something was missing because it would be so eerily quiet.

To this day I still remember when we got approved for base housing and we moved into our horror house. I remember the exact day. In fact, it was in the evening. My parents had picked up Burger King for dinner and it was awesome. I was so naïve, so young and ignorant. It was a new experience, and I had absolutely no idea as to what lay before me and my sister. It was a new home waiting to be filled with our lives. I was looking forward to meeting and making new friends despite my almost paralyzing nervousness. I never could have imagined what would happen in that house over the years.

It didn't take very long for us to move in and get into a routine. Before I knew it, I was enrolled in school—which was located on base—and began learning the lay of the land. There were really two bases in one, an old one and a new one. The original Plattsburgh Air Force Base, the old base, was built in 1955. However, everyone lived on the new side of the base and the old side seemed to be where all the servicemen and women (those who were in the military) worked.

I soon learned from the kids at school that there was some hair-standing history to the base. The old side of the base was believed to be haunted. A man's ghost supposedly lived in the gym. You were never to walk through the cemetery at night, either, because it was haunted. And there was a condemned building—which was thought to have been a hospital infirmary—that was filled with ghosts.

On the new base—in what was known as the North Side Woods—kids claimed old Farmer Brown would kidnap children who took shortcuts through the woods and they would never be seen again. And this was just the tip of the iceberg. There were stories upon stories of that place; it had loads of character.

During the War of 1812, the base at Plattsburgh came under siege by the British army led by Lieutenant General George Prévost, governor of Canada, and naval squadron Captain George Downie. His goal was to take control of Lake Champlain and lay waste to the American fleet. Plattsburgh was defended successfully by General Alexander Macomb and Master Commandant Thomas Macdonough. This event became known as the Battle of Plattsburgh, sometimes called the Battle of Lake Champlain.

All good haunting stories need a good backstory and Plattsburgh Air Force Base has one of the best. Let's be serious. What's more grueling and grim than war? There are prisoners, mutilation, wounded soldiers, torture, starvation, and, of course, death. And if that wasn't enough, in pure folklore fashion Plattsburgh is known to have its own version of the Loch Ness Monster named Champy. As a kid I remember swimming in Lake Champlain every summer. Whenever the waves suddenly picked up without a boat in sight everyone always exclaimed Champy was swimming by! We would laugh, but our laughter would ride on the back of nervousness. Plattsburgh had it all, the makings for a great thriller or a Hollywood blockbuster war movie.

My first year in Plattsburgh was exciting as well as challenging. Living as a military brat, constantly moving around, is never easy. But for the next seven years, it was our home. So I embraced it all: the lake-effect snow, the awesome four seasons, new friends, and the imaginary tales. However, little did I know I was about to learn that everything about Plattsburgh was not, in fact, imaginary.

The Plan

"In the beginning," are three words every Christian is familiar with. These words tell an entire story all by themselves and not just any story, but rather the greatest story ever told. This makes sense considering the Creator God is the greatest, maximal being to ever exist.

God developed this amazing plan for humans to bear His image as an expression of His love. Normally when you say this most believers get the warm and fuzzies because surely *we* are the primary reason for God kicking off this love story. Sorry to disappoint. Contrary to popular belief, God the Son was the primary reason (see John 17:24 and 2 Timothy 1:9). God is comprised of three persons known as a triune in nature: God the Father, God the Son, and God the Spirit. One God and three self-existing egos. Between them all is a relationship. God the Father desired to give God the Son a love gift, which was us—human beings—before the world existed. And our job is to bear His image by exercising dominion over the earth (see Genesis 1:26). However, God also clearly loves us, as displayed in John 3:16. And like all gifts the giver always desires for their gift to be perfect, whole, and complete. Not only was this the intent, it was also a reality when God created the universe and placed Adam and Eve in the Garden of Eden. In the beginning everything was good (see Genesis 1:31). What happened next was an amazingly good thing became marred with corruption.

The way the story was set to play out was Adam and Eve would tend the garden, have children, populate the earth, and enjoy God forever. Instead, we see them rebel after being tempted by one of God's creations—known as the serpent—in Genesis 3. This one act of disobedience changed the relationship between creation and man. It also changed the relationship between God and man. Not because God threw a temper tantrum as some seem to think, but because God is just and humanity was under His grace. Adam and Eve's rebellion removed them from God's grace and placed them under the law—for which they had no justification for sin. The moment they disobeyed, they had knowledge of good and evil, knowledge of sin, for which they had no recourse.

The serpent predicted this would happen the moment they ate from the tree. As soon as this event took place, Adam and Eve realized they were naked, covered their loins with fig leaves, and hid amongst the trees in the garden (see Genesis 3:7-8). The very same God they used to walk with and talk with they now feared, and they hid from Him. The relationship they once had with God had been altered. Nothing would ever be the same. What followed had crippling effects across all of creation.

After Adam and Eve sinned, God rendered a series of curses. One of them was to curse the ground (see Genesis 3:17). This curse was significant in two ways:

1) Adam, who once only had to tend creation now would have to wrestle with the earth in order to survive, only to eventually die and return back to the ground.

2) Creation, now cursed by God due to Adam's disobedience, no longer served its intended purpose. In fact, creation is now in a futile state awaiting the adoption of God's children:

For the creation waits with eager longing for the revealing of the sons of God. For the creation was subjected to futility, not willingly, but because of him who subjected it, in hope that the creation itself will be set free from its bondage to corruption and obtain the freedom of the glory of the children of God. (Romans 8:19-21)

Just as we groan and eagerly await the renewal of all things, so does creation. God's creation was intended to serve a specific purpose for mankind, but that purpose was thwarted when Adam sinned. This is a gut-wrenching but amazing thing to ponder. In all of creation's incredible wonder, intelligent design, and unparalleled order, everything is operating in futility. Why? Because, on the one hand, it is waiting for mankind to be restored back into relationship with God. On the other hand, as amazing as creation may be, we have yet to actually experience its original intent.

It is easy to think because we're dealing with God, He should have been able to just forgive and forget. But it's not a matter of power or will but of coherence. Oftentimes, especially as immature believers, we assume God can do anything when in reality He can't. God can't do things that go against His character and nature. As an example, committing sin is something God cannot do. So asking God to just forgive Adam and Eve and essentially *keep it moving*, would be like asking water to mix with oil. Logically, the natures don't allow for it. The act of disobedience had to be dealt with.

When God speaks, His words create. His action of speaking creates circumstances and scenarios that carry with it very real implications that exist beyond the physical realm. That's simply a consequence of being God. Sin is a powerful action that carries with it grave implications. Adam and Eve's act of disobedience brought a curse upon the entire universe. Every action has consequences, even metaphysically. Let us not forget that a supernatural God created an entire universe simply by speaking. This means the physical act of disobedience had to be dealt with in a supernatural way—not just in the physical sense you and I commonly think of, which would be for God's heart position to change.

But before we get too consumed with the sins of man, there's much more at play here. Adam and Eve don't have a monopoly on rebellion. Remember the serpent was also cursed. And John the revelator speaks of the dragon (Satan) being defeated in a great heavenly battle, which led to his being ousted from heaven shortly before the birth of Christ (see Revelation 12:7-8). It's also important to note that Satan wasn't alone in the war. He had a whole host of angels that were fighting against Michael's army of angels. They too were tossed out with him.

If you haven't picked up on the theme yet, there are divine beings created by God that have made it their duty to drive a wedge between man and God. Oftentimes Satan receives the full blame for the corruption of humanity, but we'll see later that he isn't alone.

I do want to be clear, though; God was *not* surprised by any of this. God is omniscient and in His omniscience He predestined a solution to the problem of a broken relationship with our Creator as well as a cursed creation. This solution lies in Jesus, the Christ (remember John 17:24 and 2 Timothy 1:9). Before God formed the world this plan was already laid out. And while this story has an amazing ending with our hero and savior—Jesus—delivering salvation to humanity, the villains known as the original sons of God still prowl around the earth.

Chapter Three

Naïve

New York was growing on me. I settled in after my first year of school. Plattsburgh is where I spent the most critical years of my youth, and, considering I was an eighties kid, I would argue that hands down my era was *the* era of all ages. I mean come on: cardboard was like gold (all of us kids used to breakdance on it). Michael Jackson was killing it. Run-D.M.C. dropped the song "My Adidas." Sony Walkman was popular. British Knights were in, and I still remember when Memorex dropped see-through cassette tapes. See-through tapes!

And don't get me started on gaming. Atari brought us Centipede, Asteroids, Dig Dug, Joust, Pitfall!, Moon Patrol, Ms. Pac-Man, and so many more games of pure awesomeness. This was a time when every other television commercial had a 1-800 call to action that sat against a blue screen with a caution for kids to first ask their parents before dialing. Millions of kids across America fell victim to the peer pressure, unable to fend off the lure to dial the number and attempt to order the latest and greatest toy. And the cartoons! Can we talk about the cartoons? *Transformers*, *ThunderCats*, He-Man, G.I. Joe, *M.A.S.K.*, *Voltron*, *Danger Mouse*, *Jayce and the Wheeled Warriors*,

Heathcliff, and *Shirt Tales*. My little sister got excited about *Jem*, *Rainbow Brite*, *Popples*, *Care Bears*, and *She-Ra*. This is just the tip of the iceberg. The eighties had everything. The eighties invented cartoons! If you ask me, the world didn't really come alive until the eighties. But I might be biased.

The eighties also taught us how to be scared. It delivered movies like *A Nightmare on Elm Street*, *Poltergeist*, *Aliens*, *Friday the 13th* and many others my parents attempted to shield me from. One of the most bone-rattling movies I saw during this time was created in the seventies. It was called *The Exorcist*. It was a movie about a girl that was demonically possessed and, let me tell you, that movie left even adults rattled. Everyone who saw that movie remembers the infamous pea soup scene. I'll spare you the gory details.

But there was something about this decade. It is arguably touted as the best decade for horror. People really wanted to be scared, and Hollywood's special effects were really taking off. But Hollywood wasn't alone, I remember Halloween becoming scarier each year as special effects improved. Frantically traversing through haunted houses made you feel like you were part of a real-life horror movie, one that you desperately wanted to get out of. We were all so naïve back then, especially me.

See, for many of us kids we desired a bit more adventure in life. Monsters, demons, spirits, witches, and warlocks seemed plausible. In fact, we believed they all existed. But believing and knowing for yourself are two different things. As I kid, I wanted to move from just hearing about these things to seeing evidence of their existence, no matter how scary they might be. Deep down inside, like most kids, and perhaps even many adults, I believed monsters might exist, but I'd never known anyone actually to be eaten by one. I never arrived at school only to find out that one of my classmates was now missing, possibly kidnapped by a witch. I didn't know anyone, nor did any of my friends know of anyone that had been possessed by a demon. So one day, I indulged myself. I decided I was going to do something different.

The Park

When I was in the fourth grade, some friends and I met up regularly after school. We usually hung out at the school park. On one occasion I was late meeting everyone. As I headed to the usual spot, I noticed the group was hunched around something. They were sitting under a tree eerily quiet, focused, concentrating on something, only to have the silence broken by gasps and laughter. When I arrived, I noticed a board with odd writing on it and two of my friends had their hands on a piece of plastic, slowly moving it around the board. At first, I thought the game was created for people absent a few screws upstairs. It wasn't until I asked what they were playing that all of that changed.

I had heard of Ouija boards (pronounced wee-gee) but never saw one in person. The board had a simple design. It was flat with the letters of the alphabet written on it. It also had the numbers 0-9, the words "Yes" and "No" and a few phrases on it. It was packaged with a white, heart-shaped piece of plastic known as a planchette with a clear center that allowed you to see what was under it. Jenna, one of the girls in my school, had been telling everyone she owned one, and of course we all thought she was lying. Jenna occasionally hung out with us at the park. That day, she brought the Ouija board, also known as a spirit board, to prove us wrong. These boards were incredibly popular in the eighties and most parents didn't let their kids play with them due to their connection with the occult. Supposedly they had the power to summon the dead simply by asking it questions. There really wasn't much to the game. We would place our fingertips on the planchette, ask the board questions and be mesmerized by the piece of plastic guiding us to the answer. We were always a bit skeptical while playing, asking each other who moved the planchette, because it couldn't have possibly moved by some sort of spiritual force. However, no one would ever confess. That would have taken the fun and mystique out of the game.

As we were playing the game, I thought, *this isn't so bad*. I had heard about how dangerous it was to play with Ouija boards, but instead of being afraid or concerned, I was excited and curious. Certainly, there was nothing to be too worried about. After all, it was made by Milton Bradley, who also sold *The Game of LIFE, Plus One*, and *Battleship*! Plus, this was the eighties! We lived to be scared by things that didn't really exist! What could possibly go wrong?

Hubris

Many people indulge themselves in horrors, testing their supposed bravery, when really deep down inside they don't believe anything demonic could ever happen to them—much like myself when I decided to indulge the Ouija board that day after school. "It's all a ruse," adults tell themselves. Figments of the imagination. "Wishful thinking from the religious zealots who aim to entrap every society on the planet with their antiquated and barbaric God-fearing belief system."

I was just like this, naïve and full of the same hubris. Since the inception of human beings, billions of people have walked the earth believing their eyes are the best source for truth. *If we see it, it must be, and if we don't, it must not be.* But humans have become really good at deception—not just at deceiving each other but even ourselves. We will twist the truth as long as it accomplishes our goals or fits a narrative we agree with. On the one hand we will claim that we must see things to believe they are true, and on the other hand we will reject this way of thinking if we don't like the end result. Our beliefs don't always align with our actions.

Take the existence of the universe for example. Many atheists will denounce the very idea of God creating the universe because they claim there is no physical evidence of God existing, meaning they haven't seen God. Yet in the same breath they will postulate that the universe could not have been created despite their never having seen how the universe came to be. *Who was actually there when it all happened?* The truth is, *seeing isn't really believing.* And so it is with the supernatural realm. Many people assume it doesn't exist because we can't see it, despite that kinda being the point. And how could we? It is *super*-natural after all. We're natural beings limited by the realities of this dimension. Our society fills up on supernatural movies and TV shows for enjoyment, but if we really believed in the demonic realm, we would not likely see it as a source of entertainment. Believers and nonbelievers alike love to indulge in all things supernatural, but if evil spirits were lurking around every corner, just as real as the sun that shines on a hot summer day, would people really continue to take them so lightly?

I saw a recent survey that reported 45 percent of Americans believe that demons and ghosts are real. Almost half of the United States believes in the supernatural. I'm willing to bet the stats would be similar for most countries. But if we truly believe in the supernatural, wouldn't our attitude about life be completely different?

The late French poet Charles Baudelaire famously wrote, "The greatest trick the devil ever pulled was convincing the world he didn't exist." How right he was. Satan, the great deceiver, managed to slip into the shadows around the time of the Renaissance period. But not only has Satan managed to slip away from our consciousness, so have the evil spirits that are commonly mentioned throughout Scripture.

The Spiritual Forces of Evil

In order for us to move forward in this book and truly understand this world, let us examine these "spiritual forces of evil" that Ephesians 6:12 mentions. Because the modern Church has traditionally concerned itself with spiritual warfare from a ten-thousand-foot view many Christians aren't able to fully grasp the nature of what is happening outside of our physical realm.

Typically, believers are taught that Satan is the leader of all demonic forces and that these forces exist to tempt humanity to sin, leading them away from God. The church has also taught that Satan was the catalyst for the corruption that has spread throughout all creation. We are taught much concerning the *evil one*, as if Satan flies solo. Many of us have learned that Satan is apparently responsible for leading one-third of the angels away from God in heaven. Then there's the whole aspect of physical manifestation of the demonic realm. When we think of demons or evil spirits—terms that are used interchangeably—we think of grotesque, vile creatures with horns, claws, and large teeth—essentially creature concepts from a Hollywood movie. Unfortunately, much of these ideas are backed by tradition not Scripture. In fact, these ideas are backed by those who've likely had no actual dealings with evil spirits. For many of you reading this, where we go from here will undoubtedly shift the way you view the world in the most dramatic sense.

The first place we need to start so we can begin to right our understanding is in the Garden of Eden. Satan is introduced as the antagonist of the story, a wicked and evil villain who has somehow snuck into the garden to deceive Eve into disobeying God. But this is a peculiar scenario that usually goes without much scrutiny from believers. There are questions we should be asking ourselves: Why was Satan in the garden to begin with? Why was Eve carrying on a conversation with him and so easily duped? Why did she seem comfortable around Satan? Why did Adam seem comfortable around Satan?

Then there's the concern of Satan's rebellion. It's commonly thought Satan was cast out of heaven before the fall due to rebellion. But if this is true, why would God give Satan access to Eden, God's special place created for His special creation? And if God cursed Satan, who was already identified as a serpent, to be a serpent slithering on its belly, then how can he transform himself to appear as an angel of light (see 2 Corinthians 11:14)? How does a serpent enter into Judas? Clearly Satan isn't confined to the nature of a snake.

These are the types of questions we're forced to ask ourselves when we no longer read Scripture through Church tradition and instead deal with the text plainly as it is. It forces us to turn on our reasoning faculties to discern exactly what Scripture is communicating. And the foundation of knowledge upon which we build becomes crucial to rightly understanding the spiritual domain and subsequently our role as humans.

The Guardian

Why was the serpent in the garden to begin with? It seems odd this evil villain would be allowed to simply waltz into Eden and strike up a conversation with Eve. It seems odd that Adam would stand next to Eve and allow this conversation to culminate into an act of willful disobedience, only to follow up with the same act.

We get a massive clue to this puzzle in the book of Ezekiel. In chapter 28 the prophet Ezekiel lays out a lament with dual meanings.

He laments over the King of Tyre's downfall, which appears to correlate with the downfall of the serpent in the garden:

Moreover, the word of the Lord came to me: "Son of man, raise a lamentation over the king of Tyre, and say to him, Thus says the Lord God: 'You were the signet of perfection, full of wisdom and perfect in beauty. You were in Eden, the garden of God; every precious stone was your covering, sardius, topaz, and diamond, beryl, onyx, and jasper, sapphire, emerald, and carbuncle; and crafted in gold were your settings and your engravings. On the day that you were created they were prepared. You were an anointed guardian cherub. I placed you; you were on the holy mountain of God; in the midst of the stones of fire you walked.'" (Ezekiel 28:11-14)

As we read these verses we can clearly see that someone else—not human—is being referenced. It is a guardian cherub placed in Eden. If you continue to read the prophecy, you'll see this guardian cherub essentially fell from God's grace and was cast low to the ground. Sound familiar?

Ezekiel's lament speaks to the beauty and wisdom of this created being. Scripture tells us he was *full* of wisdom. He was created as an anointed guardian cherub and was in Eden. We see that his nature is certainly different from man's nature. He was created as a supernatural being. God created him to be a cherub.

The first time we hear the term *cherub* is in Genesis 3:24 when Adam and Eve are kicked out of the garden and God places cherubim to guard the way to the tree of life. We see this term later in Scripture in the creation of the ark of the covenant. Moses receives instructions to include two gold cherubs at the ends of the mercy seat. It was from between the mercy seat that God would commune with Moses (see Exodus 25:22). We get a semblance of their nature from the prophet Ezekiel, who speaks of them as having wings, four faces resembling animals, and the appearance of human hands (see Ezekiel 10:1-20). They're described as "living creatures" and Ezekiel is absolutely convinced these beings were cherubim (see Ezekiel 10:20). These beings are always tied closely to the presence of God and act as some sort of guardian to things He deems as sacred.

The serpent was a cherub and Scripture makes it clear he wasn't the only one of his kind. In fact, Scripture never communicates that the serpent is unique. Ezekiel's lament continues as he describes God's judgment on the King of Tyre, which parallels the serpent's curse in the garden (see Ezekiel 28:16-19). The serpent is described as being cast out from the presence of God due to his pride. Just as he was cast to the ground, exposed for everyone to see, the King of Tyre would be exposed and shamed before other kings.

Why is all this important to know? It's vital because it helps us to understand how Eve and subsequently Adam could be so easily fooled. The serpent was a guardian cherub and one of God's most trusted divine beings. He was in Eden and, just like God, he had a relationship with man. Despite the different natures of man and God's divine beings, we were considered one family once. In fact, the serpent—who was a supernatural guardian—was never far from God. And Adam—who had dominion over the earth—walked with God. They all knew each other.

With this understanding we can see how Eve may have taken the time to listen to the serpent and become deceived. We can see how the serpent knew he could abuse Eve's trust and deceive her. This also explains how Adam could sit idly by and listen to the conversation between Eve and the serpent as it took place. Unfortunately, they failed to do what Jesus was able to accomplish: reject the tempter by standing firm in the Word of God. They failed to believe that God's words were true. Despite all God had done for them, they doubted God had their best interest in mind and reached for more.

One last thing we need to clear up is the timing of this event. Contrary to popular belief the serpent—commonly known as Satan—was not cast out of heaven just yet. As a divine being he still had access to God despite being cast out of Eden and off God's holy mountain. He lost his domain as a guardian cherub but did not lose his ability to access heaven. The book of Revelation brings this truth to light.

In John's prophecy concerning the woman and the ancient serpent, we are met with events culminating around the birth of Jesus—the one who shall rule all nations with a rod of iron and was caught up to God and His throne (see Revelation 12). In an amazing parallel, what comes next reminds us of the story of King Herod during the time of the birth of Jesus. The dragon, the ancient serpent and deceiver of the whole world, attempts to stifle God's plan by devouring the woman's child the moment it is born:

And a great sign appeared in heaven: a woman clothed with the sun, with the moon under her feet, and on her head a crown of twelve stars. She was pregnant and was crying out in birth pains and the agony of giving birth. And another sign appeared in heaven: behold, a great red dragon, with seven heads and ten horns, and on his heads seven diadems. His tail swept down a third of the stars of heaven and cast them to the earth. And the dragon stood before the woman who was about to give birth, so that when she bore her child he might devour it. She gave birth to a male child, one who is to rule all the nations with a rod of iron, but her child was caught up to God and to his throne, and the woman fled into the wilderness, where she has a place prepared by God, in which she is to be nourished for 1,260 days. (Revelation 12:1-6)

The child survives and is prophesied to rule all nations with a rod of iron. In Revelation 19 we see this same imagery which speaks to the coming Messiah. Here Jesus is described as the Rider on the White Horse, whose robe is dipped in blood, and who will strike down the nations with a *rod of iron*:

Then I saw heaven opened, and behold, a white horse! The one sitting on it is called Faithful and True, and in righteousness he judges and makes war. His eyes are like a flame of fire, and on his head are many diadems, and he has a name written that no one knows but himself. He is clothed in a robe dipped in blood, and the name by which he is called is The Word of God. And the armies of heaven, arrayed in fine linen, white and pure, were following him on white horses. From his mouth comes a sharp sword with which to strike down the nations, and he will rule them with a rod of iron. He will tread the winepress of the fury of the wrath of God the Almighty. On his robe and on his thigh he has a name written, King of kings and Lord of lords. (Revelation 19:11-16)

Immediately after the birth of the Messiah, a war in heaven breaks out. It is at this time the serpent and his angels are tossed out of heaven for warring against Michael and his angels. Scripture tells us that there was no place found for any of them.

... but he was defeated, and there was no longer any place for them in heaven. And the great dragon was thrown down, that ancient serpent, who is called the devil and Satan, the deceiver of the whole world—he was thrown down to the earth, and his angels were thrown down with him. (Revelation 12:8-9)

Immediately after the serpent and his angels are banished from heaven, there's an exultation from heaven concerning the coming kingdom of Christ:

And I heard a loud voice in heaven, saying, "Now the salvation and the power and the kingdom of our God and the authority of his Christ have come, for the accuser of our brothers has been thrown down, who accuses them day and night before our God. (Revelation 12:10)

If we think about this rationally, the order of events fits. It wouldn't make much sense for God to kick Satan out of heaven after starting a war, only to allow him into a sacred place such as Eden as a guardian cherub. But it does make sense for Satan, like Adam and Eve, to lose his rightful place but still have access to God. Satan, being a supernatural creature still had access to God. That is, until he was finally kicked out for starting a war as he attempted to thwart the coming of the Messiah. Man, who was kicked out of Eden, still had access to God through the high priests and the sacrificial system in the Old Testament.

Now that we have a better understanding of Satan, we're still left with one major unanswered question: How do the evil spirits factor into all of this? The Bible is replete with stories concerning evil or harmful spirits, but there isn't much information provided as to where they come from. The way the Bible is written it seems to assume its original audience was well aware of their origin and role within creation. The Old Testament authors appear to use the term *evil spirits* where the New Testament authors often use the term *demons*. What's even more interesting is that these evil spirits can be used by God to do His work. We see an example of this in the book of Judges concerning the downfall of Abimelech—king over Shechem, who murdered seventy of his brothers:

Abimelech ruled over Israel three years. And God sent an evil spirit between Abimelech and the leaders of Shechem, and the leaders of Shechem dealt treacherously with Abimelech, that the violence done to the seventy sons of Jerubbaal might come, and their blood be laid on Abimelech their brother, who killed them, and on the men of Shechem, who strengthened his hands to kill his brothers. And the leaders of Shechem put men in ambush against him on the mountaintops, and they robbed all who passed by them along that way. And it was told to Abimelech. (Judges 9:22-25)

Another example of this is in 1 Samuel, when God's spirit departs from Saul and immediately after God sends a harmful—evil—spirit to torment him: "Now the Spirit of the Lord departed from Saul, and a harmful spirit from the Lord tormented him" (1 Samuel 16:14).

But while we may see God sending evil spirits to inflict the wicked, it doesn't give us much information as to their origin or purpose. In order to better understand this, we will have to shed the traditional way many of us have been taught to read our Bibles and instead allow

God's word to reveal itself to us in plain language. Following this practice will open up an entirely new spiritual world for us to see and understand.

Seeing Clearly

Scripture is replete with verses that speak to the very real threat of Satan and his constant interference with God's creation and God's people, not to mention God's salvific plan. But something peculiar happened after the death of Jesus and during the mission of the apostles. The Bible's tone on Satan and demonic forces shifts from assuming the reader is aware of this supernatural evil to warning about its existence.

The book of Genesis doesn't go into great detail about the origin of Satan and what exactly happened during the rebellion. However, it speaks very matter-of-factly about Satan's existence and his interference with Eve and Adam. When Jesus arrives, Satan shows up to tempt Him. Satan tempts Peter. We see Jesus casting out demons left and right. The Pharisees claim Jesus is of the devil. Satan also shows up and enters Judas, which leads to his selling out Jesus. The Bible assumes the reader is already aware of this opponent, and while the Bible speaks explicitly in this sense, it also goes to great lengths to warn Christians to keep up their guard. Paul speaks of Satan tempting married believers if they allow for sexual deprivation (see 1 Corinthians 7:5). Paul warns us that Satan disguises himself as an angel of light (see 2 Corinthians 11:14). Peter states that we should be watchful because Satan prowls around like a lion looking for someone to devour (see 1 Peter 5:8). James speaks of resisting the devil so he will flee from you (see James 4:7). The apostle John warns us that whoever makes a practice of sinning is of the devil (see 1 John 3:8). It is clear that Satan is *the* adversary, a very present and real danger, to believers. In fact, Satan is not even a name, but a title. In Hebrew this being is actually referred to as "the satan", meaning "the adversary". Never does Scripture even hint at the possibility that Satan is no longer a threat. Yet many believers live as if he is not a big deal. Sure, we may give lip service to his existence, but our lives don't really reflect what our lips purport.

The reason many of us don't live as if Satan and his army are current threats is simply due to pride. Most Christians have been taught that Satan was defeated on the cross by Jesus. We all know the victory belongs to Christ and to us who are in Him. This very powerful truth delivers a false sense of security. This has led to ideas such as anti-biblical deliverance ministries. Not only that, but thousands of books have been written concerning how to cast out demons and how to confront Satan. Every Sunday, pastors across the world encourage their flocks to confront Satan by calling him out and mocking him—something even Michael the archangel refused to do (Jude 9).

I largely grew up in the Pentecostal church and Satan was a common subject. There he was, always interfering with every aspect of a believer's life. If you lost your job or a family member, fell ill, encountered financial troubles, got passed up for a promotion, stubbed your toe, or found a new gray hair, it was all because of Satan. Everything bad in the life of a believer was blamed on Satan, and the culpability lay with the believer who somehow opened a door to let him in. Our pride communicates to us that the great exchange that took place on the cross increased our net worth so much that nothing bad should befall us because we're saved. We forget we still sin, that the earth is still fallen, and that many of us aren't even living a life worthy of getting Satan's attention. Not to mention that he isn't omnipresent to start with.

Our view of Satan and his army becomes almost comical, like a demonic realm that more closely resembles a cast of inept characters from a fictional movie instead of a realm that even the angels have trouble with. These demonic forces have been at work for thousands of years and know their foe well. Satan and his army are able to press against the angels of heaven. Let that sink in. Angels and demons have been going at it for thousands of years and are well aware of each other's presence. You and I exist on earth for only a short lifetime. We will be lucky to see eighty years of age.

To make matters worse, we live most of our lives unaware of the spiritual war that is taking place despite our confessing to believe in demonic forces. Because of the very tainted ideas concerning the demonic realm, it is easy for us to live with a chip on our shoulders. We can find ourselves living unconcerned about this reality or puffed up in pride due to a distorted view of the spiritual realm. Both positions result in failure to understand our enemy and what is required to face him.

When I was fresh out of high school, I followed in my parent's footsteps and joined the United States Air Force. One of the most memorable things about my six weeks of boot camp—also known as basic training—was the amount of repetition and incredible amount of detail my fellow recruits and I endured. You didn't just make your bed; you had to crawl under the bed and pull the bedding so tight you could literally bounce a quarter off the mattress. You didn't just march; you had to march in perfect unison with fifty other recruits so that it sounded like one person was marching across the pavement. Everything about our lives as recruits was programmed, and it didn't stop in boot camp. Later when I arrived at my technical school in Biloxi, Mississippi, it was more of the same but with a focus on the job I was training for. When I graduated from my technical school and arrived at my first station, the training did not stop. The base where I was assigned, Seymour Johnson AFB, is part of ACC (Air Combat Command) and, because of the criticality of my job, I was required to train and test every single month just to keep my job. Throughout all of this I learned that the military recognizes the need to build what we call muscle memory. This muscle memory is necessary to ensure you stay focused on carrying out your duty regardless of the pressures—whether external or even internal—eating at you. The military can't afford for your own big-headed pride, fear, or even apathy to rule you because lives depend on your ability to do your job. It is this level of muscle memory many Christians lack today. The lack exists because many Christians today fail to recognize the reality of the threat.

In any war, in order to defeat your enemy, you must first acknowledge the existence of the enemy, and you can't be apathetic about it. You must go further than just accepting the idea of Satan or demonic forces floating in the ether. Our acceptance of the enemy's existence has to move us toward a sincere belief in the supernatural and the truths that arise from that. Like the realization that Jesus was more than just a man existing on earth, these supernatural truths should humble us. We shouldn't panic at the thought, but it should create a healthy dose of awe and fear in the incomprehensible genius of our Creator and the unknown. We would all do well to consider the words of God when He answered Job:

"Where were you when I laid the foundation of the earth? Tell me, if you have understanding. Who determined its measurements—surely you know! Or who stretched the line upon it? On what were its bases sunk, or who laid its cornerstone, when the morning stars sang together and all the sons of God shouted for joy? (Job 38:4-7)

There's a level of humility that Job had never reached until he had a conversation with God. God changed the way Job thought—not just about life but about God. Job finally confesses in Chapter 42 that he is dust and ashes. He comes to the recognition of the sheer magnitude of his own ignorance concerning the existence of all things. Job, like many of us, hit the ground running once he was born. Along the way he contrived a belief system about all that exists. This reality, for each of us, becomes based on what we can see with our own eyes. Truth is then based on what we can comprehend or test in a scientific lab. Mankind has sadly forgotten its place. It took a direct conversation with God for Job to be snapped back into reality. A reality that communicates we are but dust and ashes. A reality that informs us of how much we don't know, despite our prideful achievements. A reality that expresses the sentiment that we as humans are out of our league in this thing called life.

Chapter Four

Clockwork

I'M AWAKE. WHY AM I awake? And why do I suddenly feel sick?

I wasn't in any pain or discomfort. However, I was severely nauseous. It was the middle of the night and I made my way to the bathroom feeling as though I were about to lose everything I had for dinner. I spent the next thirty minutes having an agonizing conversation with the toilet. I was incredibly confused, lethargic, and exhausted. When I was done, I headed back to bed.

To my surprise, the following morning I felt fine. I assumed I had eaten something bad for dinner, but wondered why no one else in my family was traumatized by the 2 a.m. toilet call. I told my mother I had been sick but was doing better aside from being tired. She deemed me fit for school, because I grew up in a home where you had to be missing a limb in order to procure a sick day. I had breakfast and headed off to school not thinking too much about my night.

Thirty days later something interesting happened. I was awake once more, feeling sick to my stomach. Sitting in my room, I wondered if I was going to be sick. Yes! I darted toward the bathroom and spent the next thirty minutes having another conversation with the toilet. *What is going on? What did I eat?* Here I was again, sick to my stomach, losing everything I ate for dinner. When I was done, I headed back to bed. The next morning I was tired but felt well enough to eat and go to school. I told my mom I had been sick, but I didn't have any symptoms. I went to school and didn't think too much about what was occurring.

Fast-forward thirty days and yet again I had another late-night debate with the toilet while the rest of the house was dead sleep. Not only did this event catch my attention, but it had become a bit more violent and unrelenting. What was thirty minutes in the bathroom had become an hour stint. Once I was done, I headed back to my room, climbed into my bed, and just lay there. I couldn't figure out why this was happening to me or what was going on. Was it some fluke or would it come again to interrupt my night? *And why the hell was nobody else sick?!*

The next morning I was wrecked. I felt like a train hit me from being up all night losing every bit of nutrition my body had. I didn't feel like eating, but due to having zero symptoms I wasn't able to secure a stay-at-home card from my mother. This was becoming very odd. I needed to figure it out.

Every thirty days like clockwork I would wake up and vomit. I first started suspecting the food my parents were cooking, but it was never the same meal that caused me to be sick. Plus, everyone else in the home was eating the same meal. I then suspected it was the water fountain at school, so I stopped drinking from it. Nothing changed. I wasn't done yet, though, because clearly it had to be something I was ingesting.

My sister and I would often drink water out of the bathroom sink because my mom had conveniently installed a cup dispenser on the wall. It was mainly for rinsing our mouths out when we brushed our teeth in the morning, but we also used the cups to drink water throughout the day. The base we lived on was notorious for having brown water at times, so I thought it was possible that I was drinking this water when the pipes were being cleared out. So I doubled down on inspecting the water, filling up the sink or tub to see if there was any brown in the water at all. If it was crystal clear, it got my approval to drink. However, this didn't stop the late-night attacks, so I conceded just to stop drinking water from the sink altogether. Still, nobody else was getting sick at night.

I wasn't done yet. I figured the next time I woke up and felt sick I would just hold it all in and become the victor. Nothing was going to stop me from winning this battle. Little did I realize that God designed other ways for things to leave the head in the event the mouth would not open. Let's just say it wasn't a good experience. That next morning, not only did I feel defeated, but my entire nasal cavity was on fire.

This went on for years. Every. Single. Month. After three weeks without getting sick in the middle of the night, it became a waiting game. A few times I made it through four weeks and would think I had finally kicked this thing—whatever it was. However, it would always manage to emerge and get the last laugh.

This wasn't the worst of it though. Yes, you heard me right. This was *not* the worst of what was going on in my life. When this sickness showed up, I started having what I thought were bad dreams—until

I realized I wasn't asleep when some very real and scary things started happening to me at night.

It had been years since the incident with the thundering closet. In fact, I had forgotten all about it. One of the blessings of early childhood is the ability to forget, especially things that are traumatic. However, it seems that the older we get the more difficult it becomes to forget. Furthermore, one of the curses of being a child is the inability to always discern what's real from what isn't, as a result of an overactive imagination compounded with the fact that everything in the world is still new. Is Willy Wonka's chocolate factory actually real? Why can't reindeer fly if Santa can use magic? Why can't fire-breathing dragons exist if dinosaurs once existed? What child never dreams up Goonies-type fantasies of having the most lenient parents on earth, a pack of cool friends, and the chance to thwart danger with them in search of haunted, buried treasure? And what kid doesn't believe in ghosts, witches, ghouls, and spirits? As a child you almost *want* to experience supernatural events despite being terrified by them—the things that make Halloween terribly fun and graveyards risky to run through at night. As a child you almost expect to experience something supernaturally evil at least once in your life. In fact, this is a good time to tell you about my Bloody Mary stint.

When I was just six years old, I decided I was going to play a game of Bloody Mary in the Mirror with a bunch of friends while at summer camp. At the time, Bloody Mary was all the rage. The story behind the game is that if you called Bloody Mary in a mirror three times with the lights off, she would appear and kill you. Sounds fun, right? *Yep, we were stupid.*

So there we were. Eleven of us conspired to take over a boy's bathroom and play our little game once it became vacant. When we found an opening, we made our way into the bathroom, closed the door, and shut off the lights. I remember the exhaust fan still running after the lights were turned off. It was loud and obnoxious. A few of the kids stood by the door claiming to keep watch in case one of the summer camp assistants tried to intrude and ruin our fun. But really those boys were trying to position themselves to be first out of the bathroom in the event Bloody Mary made an actual appearance. Some of my friends just stood in the center of the bathroom, completely giddy with pent up anxiety. I bravely stood in front of the mirror with a couple of my buds to chant the name of Bloody Mary to see what would happen. If she was real, I wanted to see her face. My expectations consisted of us kids scaring each other and running out frantically. Well, part of my expectations was met.

We started off slow, giggling and building up our courage, "Bloody Mary ... Bloody Mary." Then we started getting brave and louder. We were almost daring her to show up. Louder we became with the chant and faster, calling her name, "Bloody Mary, Bloody Mary, Bloody Mary!" Then out of nowhere we heard a loud POP! The exhaust fan came to a screeching halt, as if something was jammed inside of it. The lights wouldn't turn on, and the door wouldn't open. Somehow it was locked from the inside. I watched several of my friends attempt to open the door. The giddy, brave laughter turned to panicky, girl-like screaming. I swear someone peed on the floor. Some of the kids started pounding on the door, yelling for someone to open it. The rest of us were either holding our ears and screaming or holding each other and screaming. After what seemed like an eternity in blackness, stuck in the bathroom with Bloody Mary, the door opened, and one of the camp assistants asked us what was going on. In between her laughs she scolded us for playing in the bathroom, but I don't think any of us actually heard what she said because we were too busy tearing out of there as if it were on fire. Needless to say, we never, *ever* played that game again. I'm now a grown man and, even though I don't believe in Bloody Mary in the Mirror, I'm still too emotionally scarred to even attempt it again—that was an epic shot at my manhood at the age of six.

Just a couple of years later I had forgotten all of this. It was just another hiccup in the space-time continuum. After moving to Plattsburgh, the new occurrences—the bumps in the night, the so-called *night terrors* of children who are thought to have overactive imaginations—jolted my memory. Never does it cross your mind to think about *where* these terrible ideas come from or why they exist. We are all told these ghosts or demons either come directly from a place called hell, or they're spirits who are trapped on earth and have nothing better to do than terrorize the living. Either way, as the stories go, they're all evil, and they do not like humans for some odd reason.

Evil Spirits

Between the inception of the early church and today something has changed. That *something* is the church's perception of creation as well as its understanding of the wicked spiritual forces at play. If you were to ask about the origin of evil spirits or demons, most believers would not be able to give an answer. If you're lucky, you may get a response that they are fallen angels. This isn't accurate, but at least it's in the ballpark as far as a biblical answer goes. Personally, I find that concerning but also odd. What's even more odd is the Bible doesn't lay out a verse with a clear answer to their origin.

Somewhere within the timeline of church history the definition of evil spirits became obfuscated. Events such as the great war in heaven—recorded in Revelation 12—are now interpreted by many as the fallen angels are evil spirits or demons. But as we'll see, Scripture doesn't support that interpretation. In fact, what happened to the fallen angels and the idea of them turning into evil spirits is not what took place.

For all the emphasis on the demonic realm, you would think Scripture would—at a minimum—explain how evil spirits originated. Because this information seems to be absent one could simply conclude that it isn't important. Or one could take a different approach and conclude that the writers of the Bible wrote with an assumption that we should already know the answer to the riddle. And why would they do that?

Unfortunately, most believers have been taught not to question things of great biblical importance—at least not too deeply. But this highlights the issue of blindly following church tradition. While the Bible is most certainly sufficient for salvation and completely inerrant, it is fair to acknowledge that the Bible does not detail everything that has ever taken place since God first spoke creation into existence. And that's okay. That isn't the purpose of the Bible. Too often we ascribe purpose to Scripture that was simply never intended. However, because scrutinizing the Bible is pretty taboo, believers often fail to consume what could be incredibly helpful material out of fear of being called a heretic. If we simply look back to what the early church thought about the demonic, we'd be quite surprised at the chasm that now exists between us and the early saints.

One of our early church fathers, Tertullian, had much to say concerning the demonic realm. In his book *Apology*, he states that the belief in demons was very widespread. Not only was the belief widespread, it was not *exclusive* to believers:

And we affirm indeed the existence of certain spiritual essences; nor is their name unfamiliar. The philosophers acknowledge there are demons; Socrates himself waiting on a demon's will. Why not? Since it is said an evil spirit attached itself specially to him even from his childhood—turning his mind no doubt from what was good. The poets are all acquainted with demons too; even the ignorant common people make frequent use of them in cursing. In fact, they call upon Satan, the demon-chief, in their execrations, as though from some instinctive soul-knowledge of him. Plato also admits the existence of angels. The dealers in magic, no less, come forward as witnesses to the existence of both kinds of spirits. (Apology, Ch. 22)[1]

It is clear that the belief in demons and angels didn't come to an abrupt halt once Christ ascended to the throne. Tertullian is taking the time not just to proclaim that *he* believes in this spiritual realm, but rather *all* people have become acquainted with it even if they don't fully understand what's happening. He adds that some have what appears to be inherent knowledge of these evils. He begins by stating a collective affirmation of this truth, which would consist of the church. He then identifies philosophers, poets, those involved in witchcraft, and even common people who are ignorant of the spiritual realm. This simply builds off what we've seen in Scripture from the Old Testament to the New Testament. Tertullian is merely carrying on this truth. He then goes a step further and presents information as to the origin of such beings:

We are instructed, moreover, by our sacred books how from certain angels, who fell of their own free-will, there sprang a more wicked demon-brood, condemned of God along with the authors of their race, and that chief we have referred to. (Apology, Ch. 22)[2]

In this one succinct sentence, Tertullian lays out for us the origin of the demonic realm along with other important facts.

To start, he mentions sacred books, plural. (In order to be brief and less academic, we will focus on just one of those books. For

---

1. Tertullian, Apology, Chap. 22, newadvent.org, https://www.newadvent.org/fathers/0301.htm.

2. Ibid.

a more exhaustive study on this topic, I recommend Dr. Michael S. Heiser's *The Unseen Realm*.) The book I'd like to focus on is 1 Enoch, also known as the *Book of Enoch*. Now, as someone who has been a Christian for quite some time, I know the knee-jerk reaction many believers have when they hear that book. They hiss, gasp, or scream *heresy* at the top of their lungs toward any book that is not in the Bible. I believe that's an unfortunate consequence of the manner in which many of us came to learn about the Christian faith. In fact, I believe the church would be stronger if all believers learned more about the early church and its fathers. To be clear, I am not suggesting that extra-biblical texts *are* or *should* be considered Scripture. I am not advocating that the *Book of Enoch* should be considered Scripture. I *am* advocating that we as believers need to better understand which extra-biblical texts may provide additional context to the faith and which ones we should avoid entirely. *The Book of Enoch*—while not Scripture—is *not* considered heretical or a work of fiction. It is considered to be part of pseudepigrapha works—works most likely not written by the named author. The early church fathers as well as the authors of the Bible didn't start from blank slates. It is important to remember that the writers of the Bible drew from other sources in order to complete their work that was guided by the Spirit of God. Two examples we can use as proof come from the second letter of Peter and the letter of Jude.

Peter alludes to the same event as Tertullian concerning fallen angels that were condemned by God: "For if God did not spare angels when they sinned, but cast them into hell and committed them to chains of gloomy darkness to be kept until the judgment …" (2 Peter 2:4). Jude corroborates this story:

And the angels who did not stay within their own position of authority, but left their proper dwelling, he has kept in eternal chains under gloomy darkness until the judgment of the great day—just as Sodom and Gomorrah and the surrounding cities, which likewise indulged in sexual immorality and pursued unnatural desire, serve as an example by undergoing a punishment of eternal fire. (Jude 6-7)

What is interesting about Jude is that he goes a step further and describes the angels' actual sin. He mentions they left their proper position and dwelling. Another way of thinking about this is that the angels left the domain over which they had authority. Jude continues into verse 7 and compares the sin of the angels to the sin of Sodom and Gomorrah—which was the sin of sexual immorality. And like those of Sodom and Gomorrah, these angels will face eternal fire as punishment.

Thus far we've been able to corroborate this one event between Tertullian, Peter, and Jude. The last piece of the puzzle centers around what Enoch—great-grandfather of Noah—captured concerning the fallen angels:

And it came to pass when the children of men had multiplied that in those days were born unto them beautiful and comely daughters. And the angels, the children of the heaven, saw and lusted after them, and said to one another: 'Come, let us choose us wives from among the children of men and beget us children.' And Semjaza, who was their leader, said unto them: 'I fear ye will not indeed agree to do this deed, and I alone shall have to pay the penalty of a great sin.' And

they all answered him and said: 'Let us all swear an oath, and all
bind ourselves by mutual imprecations not to abandon this plan but
to do this thing.' Then sware they all together and bound themselves
by mutual imprecations upon it. And they were in all two hundred;
who descended in the days of Jared on the summit of Mount Hermon,
and they called it Mount Hermon, because they had sworn and bound
themselves by mutual imprecations upon it. And these are the names
of their leaders: Semiazaz, their leader, Arakiba, Rameel, Kokabiel,
Tamiel, Ramiel, Danel, Ezeqeel, Baraqijal, Asael, Armaros, Batarel,
Ananel, Zaqiel, Samsapeel, Satarel, Turel, Jomjael, Sariel. These are
their chiefs of tens. (Book of Enoch, Ch. 6)[3]

Enoch seems to have what appears to be firsthand knowledge of
what took place. He provides additional detail, which corroborates
what Tertullian, Peter, and Jude wrote. Now here's where things
become really exciting or terrifying, depending on how you look at
it. The fall of the angels—otherwise known as sons of God—was
recorded in the book of Genesis. This event is often glossed over
because it is outweighed by the sins of Adam and Eve and also
because much context has been left out. However, it is a major event
that took place soon after the fall of Adam:

When man began to multiply on the face of the land and daughters
were born to them, the sons of God saw that the daughters of man were
attractive. And they took as their wives any they chose. Then the Lord
said, "My Spirit shall not abide in man forever, for he is flesh: his days

---

3. The Book of Enoch, Sacred-Texts.com,
   https://www.sacred-texts.com/bib/boe/boe009.htm.

shall be 120 years." The Nephilim were on the earth in those days, and also afterward, when the sons of God came in to the daughters of man and they bore children to them. These were the mighty men who were of old, the men of renown. (Genesis 6:1-4)

Now that we've connected the dots, we can easily see that Genesis 6, Tertullian, Jude, and Peter all speak to the same event that concerns a group of angels who left their domain. But I want to highlight another critical piece that Tertullian identified, the demon-brood. A brood is commonly defined as a young animal or a family of young animals, oftentimes used to describe the offspring of birds. Tertullian makes a point to call out a certain type of offspring—a demonic offspring now existing within the earth.

After the sons of God left their domain by exercising sexual immorality with the women on earth, the women gave birth to the Nephilim, which are known as giants. The *Book of Enoch* purports that soon after this event the earth became corrupt. Not only did the sons of God alter humanity through sexual immorality, but the giants ended up eating everything that men produced and then turned on mankind by eating them to survive. Apparently even this wasn't enough because they then began to cannibalize one another. God then commissioned Noah to build an ark so that his family would be saved. At this point, all flesh had become corrupt. What was happening on the earth was akin to a plague running rampant.

Now the earth was corrupt in God's sight, and the earth was filled with violence. And God saw the earth, and behold, it was corrupt, for all flesh had corrupted their way on the earth. (Genesis 6:11-12)

We find this same story in the *Book of Enoch* but with a bit more detail:

Then said the Most High, the Holy and Great One spake, and sent Uriel to the son of Lamech, and said to him: "Go to Noah and tell him in my name 'Hide thyself!' and reveal to him the end that is approaching: that the whole earth will be destroyed, and a deluge is about to come upon the whole earth, and will destroy all that is on it. And now instruct him that he may escape and his seed may be preserved for all the generations of the world." And again the Lord said to Raphael: "Bind Azazel hand and foot, and cast him into the darkness: and make an opening in the desert, which is in Dudael, and cast him therein. And place upon him rough and jagged rocks, and cover him with darkness, and let him abide there for ever, and cover his face that he may not see light. And on the day of the great judgement he shall be cast into the fire. And heal the earth which the angels have corrupted, and proclaim the healing of the earth, that they may heal the plague, and that all the children of men may not perish through all the secret things that the Watchers have disclosed and have taught their sons. And the whole earth has been corrupted through the works that were taught by Azazel: to him ascribe all sin." (Book of Enoch, Ch. 10:1-9)[4]

You probably didn't learn that in Sunday school, did you? If you're like me, you may have wondered precisely *how* the earth was corrupted so badly that God would have to literally wipe it clean

---

4. The Book of Enoch, Sacred-Texts.com,
   https://www.sacred-texts.com/bib/boe/boe013.htm.

with a flood. But what we still don't know is precisely *where* the demons came from. Enoch once again gives us this information by revealing that these evil spirits are the offspring of the giants that were born on earth:

And now, the giants, who are produced from the spirits and flesh, shall be called evil spirits upon the earth, and on the earth shall be their dwelling. Evil spirits have proceeded from their bodies; because they are born from men and from the holy Watchers is their beginning and primal origin. (Book of Enoch, Ch. 15:8-9)[5]

We see that the wicked giants were considered evil spirits due to their divine but human nature and from them evil spirits would proceed. This would take effect once God killed all of creation as their spirits would be trapped on earth. Again, Enoch reveals this and also the purpose of these spirits.

They shall be evil spirits on earth, and evil spirits shall they be called. As for the spirits of heaven, in heaven shall be their dwelling, but as for the spirits of the earth which were born upon the earth, on the earth shall be their dwelling. And the spirits of the giants afflict, oppress, destroy, attack, do battle, and work destruction on the earth, and cause trouble: they take no food, but nevertheless hunger and thirst, and cause offences. And these spirits shall rise up against the children of men and against the women, because they have proceeded from them. (Book of Enoch, Ch. 15:9-11)[6]

---

5. The Book of Enoch, Sacred-Texts.com,
   https://www.sacred-texts.com/bib/boe/boe018.htm.

6. Ibid.

Tertullian must have also read *The Book of Enoch* as he agrees with this claim in his *Apology*, Chapter 22.

Their great business is the ruin of mankind. So, from the very first, spiritual wickedness sought our destruction. They inflict, accordingly, upon our bodies diseases and other grievous calamities, while by violent assaults they hurry the soul into sudden and extraordinary excesses. Their marvellous subtleness and tenuity give them access to both parts of our nature.[7]

It is at this point that I would be remiss not to point us towards what Ephesians 6 says to make all of this a bit more salient and real.

For we do not wrestle against flesh and blood, but against the rulers, against the authorities, against the cosmic powers over this present darkness, against the spiritual forces of evil in the heavenly places. (Ephesians 6:12)

This verse is *one* of the most powerful and enlightening verses in all of Scripture. Unfortunately, it's not treated as such. While this verse is incredibly popular among Christians, many Christians don't know what it means, like an untrained soldier being deployed to war. Sure, an untrained solder who sprays enough bullets may hit something, including their own eye, but without proper combat training and an understanding of your enemy, you'll be the most ineffective soldier in the field. The reason I say this is because many Christians don't know the origin story as to how evil and demonic

---

7. Tertullian, Apology, Chap. 22, newadvent.org,
   https://www.newadvent.org/fathers/0301.htm.

forces infiltrated the earth. In fact, *most people* in general don't know this origin story.

And what an amazing story it is! When you begin to realize the full scope of created beings, the original interplay, and our relationships as one family, we can see God through a much wider, clearer lens. What we see within the creation story is the establishment of family—a family that includes diverse beings that express God's creativity, love, and power. Soon after creation we see something that is tantamount to sibling rivalry on steroids, which destroyed the very nature of what relationship should be. It marred the very essence of what family *should* be. To make this a little more practical, in Sun Tzu's *The Art of War* we find this:

"Hence the saying: If you know the enemy and know yourself, you need not fear the result of a hundred battles. If you know yourself but not the enemy, for every victory gained you will also suffer a defeat. If you know neither the enemy nor yourself, you will succumb in every battle."[8]

If we're going to be most effective in this world with the time God has given us, then we need to understand the landscape. It is not enough to know demons and Satan exist. We need to be able to answer why, who, where, and what. With a clearer understanding of the relationship between the beings that God created, we can better navigate the enemy's territory. We can begin to see and understand the things taking place around us using true spiritual discernment.

---

8. Sun Tzu, The Art of War, Ch. 3, v. 18,
   https://suntzusaid.com/book/3/18.

This discernment isn't offered to those who are lost and without Christ:

See to it that no one takes you captive by philosophy and empty deceit, according to human tradition, according to the elemental spirits of the world, and not according to Christ. (Colossians 2:8)

This discernment gives us the ability to lift the veil covering the eyes of the world. We see what the world can't.

As my children grow up, one of the things I press into their minds almost daily is that the world is not what it seems. There are domains within our reality that, while we may not be able to see them physically, are much closer to us than we realize. The impact from the spiritual realm is constant, usually while we're unaware of the assaults. Let me paint a picture.

Like most children, I spent a lot of time playing outdoors near dense, wooded areas. When I would come in for the night, I was always astonished by the number of mosquito bites I had received. I was intrigued, to say the least. *How were they so attracted to people? Why were they attracted? And why couldn't I feel them?* It wasn't until later in life that I learned some startling facts about mosquitos.

First, mosquitos are attracted to carbon dioxide and lactic acid. Simply breathing and going about our lives attracts their attention—just like demons. Another unsettling fact about mosquitoes is that their mouths are so tiny you can't feel them biting into your flesh and injecting their saliva, which includes an anesthetic, into your skin. This is the reason you can't feel them until it's too late, if at all. With your skin numbed, they then begin to feed, drawing your life's blood into their bodies. This is no different than the evil spirits prowling around, seeking whom they will devour. It isn't until later that we begin to physically feel the impacts rippling through our lives. Usually, completely unaware of the assault that took place, we reel from the piercings of our flesh and feel the repercussions in a number of different ways.

These attacks are precisely what our early church father Tertullian wrote about. He certainly was convinced of the existence of spiritual evils within our world. And he wasn't alone. Tertullian references the same fallen sons account of which both Jude and Peter write. Their accounts are derived from what Enoch experienced. Through this account we now have a better understanding as to the causes of the earth's corruption. We can also rightly lay blame on the appropriate offenders for their actions. While Satan is culpable for deceiving Adam and Eve—thereby introducing sin followed by humanity falling out of relationship with God—Azazel, the leader of the fallen sons, is culpable for corrupting the entire earth. While Azazel—and the other Watchers—are bound within the earth, Satan, along with the demonic spirits, is still free.

These spirits have one aim, which is to lead humanity away from God. And, this aim isn't born out of boredom or because God created certain beings to be just diabolically evil. This wickedness is perpetuated by jealousy of the human race, which is compounded by pride. When we look around at the sinfulness of man, it can be difficult to understand what makes us so special. One of David's Psalms helps us out:

When I look at your heavens, the work of your fingers, the moon and the stars, which you have set in place, what is man that you are mindful of him, and the son of man that you care for him? Yet you have made him a little lower than the heavenly beings and crowned him with glory and honor. You have given him dominion over the works of your hands; you have put all things under his feet, all sheep and oxen, and also the beasts of the field, the birds of the heavens, and the fish of the sea, whatever passes along the paths of the seas. (Psalm 8:3–8)

Despite being created just a little lower than the heavenly beings, Scripture says we are crowned with God's glory and honor. Us. Humans. Like the heavenly and divine beings God created, we too were given dominion, but our dominion is all of creation. Let that sink in. How awesome is our God! How generous, gracious, and loving is our God! For He has given us—those created from the dust with no special abilities and no heavenly attributes or divine powers—dominion over *His* creation.

Is it no wonder that sibling rivalry exists between us and certain heavenly beings God created? And at the center of this spiritual war is a catalyst called pride—the same sinful desire that even humanity cannot escape, which is: the desire to be like God instead of staying within our own domain.

Chapter Five

The House Speaks

DURING MY YOUNGER AND more naïve years, I was a pretty big fan of horror movies. I'm not sure if I just had some weird genetic disposition towards them, or if I was simply a byproduct of the '80s. Horror movies were nothing I really ever sought after, I just found something compelling about them as a child—the outlandish plots, bad animatronics, and fake blood. While movies such as *A Nightmare on Elm Street, Halloween,* and *Friday the 13th* were creepy, they couldn't hold a candle to the more plausible movies involving haunted homes and seemingly normal people. Don't get me wrong. The character of Freddy Krueger was an incredible stroke of genius and caused many people to dread closing their eyes at night. But nobody really believed he could exist and kill you twice: in your dream and in real life. To this day, people still debate if *Halloween* was better than *Friday the 13th.* But really, who's expecting a Jason Voorhees (*Friday the 13th*) or Michael Myers (*Halloween*) slasher to show up on their doorstep, in their backseat, or at their school? These movies are *almost* too unbelievable. But movies like *House, Poltergeist,* and the 1973 film *The Exorcist,* are far more harrowing. These movies invade your soul because there is an element of realness to them that you can't quite put your finger on. That element is demonic activity and possession.

I've learned the fear of the unknown is only half as scary as the fear of the known-*but*-unseen. How do you reconcile the ideas of demons inhabiting people and places, lurking around corners, watching you, having conversation with you through others, and inflicting harm without your awareness? These evil spirits have set their sights on harming mankind without tipping their hand. They are beyond cunning. They have convinced people they don't exist. To encounter demonic activity causes our senses to wage war against our mind, which tries to latch on to whatever sanity we have left.

During my childhood, I started to think I was going insane. No child should have to go through that. The only relief I had was the fact that I was asking the question. Perhaps asking myself if I was crazy was a sign that I hadn't yet totally lost my mind. Or maybe I was just in the process of losing it.

Darkness

It started slowly. I woke up in the middle of the night while my family was fast asleep. The silence was beyond deafening. I wasn't sure why I was fully awake, but there I was, lying flat on my stomach. Then I sensed it. Something was in my room. I was filled with sheer terror as I came to grips with a sense of pure evil surrounding me. It was this evil that woke me up. I closed my eyes out of panic and pretended to be asleep. I could feel it moving across my bedroom. Not walking, or sliding, no, just moving. Whatever it was, I could feel it moving closer to me, just like the incident I experienced when I was much younger. I was paralyzed by fear. As I lay there, it loomed over me. Staring. Waiting. Then slowly, it grabbed me underneath my armpits. I was petrified. It felt like hands but not like hands. Never in my life had I experienced a sensation such as this. I wanted to get away. I would have died if I could have. I could think of nothing else but to pretend I was asleep. To play dead. To lie motionless. Not even to breathe. I could feel it close to me. But there was no breath. No body heat or smells. It was holding me, staring at me, almost contemplating something. Then, it let me go. Hands slid from under my armpits and then it went back to wherever it came from. Needless to say, I didn't go back to sleep that night. *What in the bloody hell?* Literally!

I know many people who find these types of experiences unbelievable. Some may claim I was a victim of sleep paralysis—a sleep disorder that causes its victim to wake up temporarily paralyzed. Sometimes when one experiences sleep paralysis, one can also experience hallucinations. Much has been written on this subject. To be fair, I actually do suffer from sleep paralysis. I've had it my entire life. As an adult, I still experience it. However, being burdened with sleep paralysis my entire life means I know fully what it is and what it isn't. I know what it is to be fully awake and yet unable to move my body, trapped. I also know what it is to hallucinate while experiencing an episode. Even today, when I experience an episode, I usually wake my wife as I repeatedly wiggle any body part that will respond—a finger, a toe, a click with my tongue. I know she's next to me. I can sense her. My wife then awakens and shakes me, which is enough to snap me out of it. I can feel her when she touches me. I know what sleep paralysis is. I know what it isn't. And I'm aware of the stories about old hags and evil spirits that sit on your chest, which are apparent hallucinations.

The evil I felt that night while my family slept was not an episode of sleep paralysis. No old hags or witches sitting on my chest, holding me down. I could actually move, but I chose not to out of sheer terror. I didn't even attempt to move. In fact, I was trying not to move, not to scream, not to outwardly panic, while inside I was erupting in dread. I remember thinking that if I appeared to be asleep, then it would leave me alone. But if I did anything contrary, it could be a long night. And just the very thought of opening my eyes to meet this evil was enough to make me want to die. This is not sleep paralysis. In fact, as horrible as sleep paralysis is, I would have traded it a million times over for the experience I just had.

Unfortunately, these visits became a common occurrence. In the beginning I kept them to myself, thinking they would eventually go away. Thinking, maybe I was imagining it all. *These have to be nightmares of a different kind. They'll stop eventually. Yeah, they'll stop. I must be losing it.*

But they didn't. I mentioned these visits to my parents, who seemed unimpressed. If anything, they were convinced my episodes were my sins coming back to haunt me. As a child, I believed their theory. Do bad things as a kid and the monsters come and get you. But did they really believe that? I have no idea. Their reaction offered zero solace for my distress, though. Now it just sounds like some sort of ancient Black folklore.

Around the age of twelve, my life was hell. The vomiting became worse and more aggressive. The sickness attacks lasted longer. At times I would empty my stomach only to be met with what looked like my insides cased in blood. I would be horrified. I would find myself on the floor praying for the agony to stop. By morning it was always like it had never happened. In the morning my mom would shrug her shoulders while looking confused. "See, nothing wrong," she'd say, while giving me the usual dose of Pepto-Bismol and then sending me to school.

Nearly every week I was being visited by some manner of evil that I couldn't put into words. I was terrified to go to sleep for what might wake me. Scared to be awake at night, because I knew the bathroom toilet was waiting for me. And I was alone. The quiet and peaceful nights I used to know were no longer to be found.

I longed for school. School? Yes. It was the one place I felt safe. No sickness and no evil spirits. But as I went about my day, the terror awaiting me sat at the back of my mind. Every day as I talked with friends, enjoyed gym class, and dug into my assignments, I was counting down the hours. By nightfall I was nervous. Who can stop the night? For it comes swiftly, diligently, and with purpose like oxygen to the lungs.

When I closed my eyes for the evening, there I was, often lying on my back staring down at the foot of my bed. I used to wake up and see the back of my door, because I always kept it closed. That changed. I started to sleep with the door open, as I had become terrified of being trapped in my room with this evil. I thought I might get lucky and someone would pass by my room and rescue me from this evil. Then they would know I wasn't crazy because they would see it too! But this evil was all too cunning. Its timing was perfect, never to be caught or outdone. It always attacked at the witching hour, the time when demonic activity is at its height. I don't know if the witching hour is real or not. All I knew at the time was that nothing was going to catch this spirit in action.

I would awaken at random times throughout the night because I was too afraid to sleep. Staring towards the foot of my bed, into the darkness which was the stairway across the hallway, I would lay there waiting. Listening. And just when I thought it couldn't get any worse, the steps on the stairway started creaking.

When I heard the first creak, I assumed it was the house settling. I'd often hear odd noises even during the day. Plattsburgh, New York, brought some brutal winters and oddly some incredibly hot summers. So it was common to hear pipes and windows cracking and popping all the time. But this sound coming from the stairway was heavy. It wasn't a pop or a crack. There was some weight behind it. I tried to shrug it off, but then there was another step. I stared into the darkness from my bed, hoping it was one of my family members playing a trick on me in the dark. But I knew that was me trying to cope. No one was there. Everyone was sleep! Minutes would go by, and I would hear it again—the floor creaking under pressure. I could hear it getting closer. I would then hear this pressing in the hallway in front of my room, right in my doorway. Then it would return to the steps. Like something was standing guard in front of my room. After a while, it would stop. Like it had never happened.

And so it is with demonic activity. I learned at an early age that it isn't like in the movies. Demonic activity doesn't typically show up in the middle of the day, well-announced, proclaiming its evilness from the rooftops for all to see. We all know a magician never reveals his or her tricks. When in enemy territory a soldier never reveals his identity. This level of strategic operation is why many people have absolutely no clue as to what really exists in this world. It is precisely why so many people don't believe in supernatural evil. Is it possession or a mental disorder? Can it be both? Are you really experiencing the supernatural, or maybe it's your brain projecting a false reality? What better way to subvert your enemy than with subterfuge from within their own camp?

My house wasn't safe, and I hated living in it. I hated everything about it. To this day I still have dreams about being stuck in that wretched house. The way it smelled. The sounds it made when you walked on the floor. Nothing felt right in the home—not even the relationships I had with my parents or my sister. I only remember pain and suffering. Living in that house taught me what it meant to be alone and terrified. Memories of my old home in Plattsburgh are never without the evil that filled it.

Be Brave

I had a book of fables and in it was a picture of the devil—you know, the red devil that has horns and hooves for feet. According to this book, one way to tell if he had visited your town was by looking for hoofprints. And, since the devil walks upright, you would see only two. In fact, during the winter months, each morning I would stare out my window after a fresh snow to see if I could find any signs of these tracks, signs that the devil was real, so I could use that as evidence for my parents. Needless to say, I never found any tracks. Sounds crazy, doesn't it? Yeah, well, this was how far my mind was being stretched.

One evening—as I sifted through this book of evil characters—I came to the end of my rope. I had had enough. I was tired of the visits. I was angry, and as I sat there staring at this red, half human, half goat-like creature with a beard, my blood boiled. It was like he was laughing at me, enjoying the torment. His nasty grin and bulging eyes were seeking his next victim. I was raging on the inside, and I let it out. I started swearing at my enemy in this book. I punched his face until my hands started to bruise. No swear word was off-limits. I closed the book and tossed it. It would be the last time I ever opened that book. If you're wondering why, I'll explain.

Later that night I hopped in the bed feeling a bit more confident than normal. My sleeping habits had evolved. I had started laying a second blanket over my feet and pulling it tight underneath the mattress. The security of practically tying my feet down made me feel better protected. I would also tuck the rest of my blanket in up to my arms so nothing could reach me underneath the sheets. I basically had to slide under my covers in order to get in bed. This cocoon gave me a lot of comfort. Nothing could touch me. Or so I thought!

I closed my eyes and went to sleep. When I awoke, I was already in his hands. The energy was different. It was angrier, and it squeezed me harder than it ever had—like it was proving a point. I remember being uncomfortable and squirming, yet it wouldn't let me go. Normally I would play dead so the visit could be over, but this time I was angry too. I could see nothing as I was face down and trapped. I felt like I was falling while still being held. I wanted to get away! But not like before. I was in so much torment I regretted angering the spirit. I gave up my fight and learned in that moment that there was an agreement. It would torment me when it chose, and I had better accept it. Then, it was gone.

I opened my eyes. I was dejected. Whatever spirit I had left was broken. I was so distraught I couldn't cry. I felt pain, fear, despair, and anger all at once with no avenue to release any of it. Whom could I tell? My parents didn't believe me. They just shrugged it off like most parents. Like most people. They hear you tell your story, but they don't *listen* to your story. It's as if you're talking to a pet. They'll acknowledge the conversation, but, really, if it doesn't affect them, they couldn't care less. And since they never experienced it, it must not really be happening. But if it were happening, what was anyone going to do about it?

Float

The spirit in our house wasn't happy. At least it certainly wasn't happy with me. Whenever I thought the experiences couldn't get any worse, I was unfortunately surprised.

I began to waken in the middle of the night to untucked blankets. I was exposed, as my cocoon had unraveled. I would quickly sit up and fix them. Extra blanket tucked over feet. Place additional pillow on feet if I must. Sides tucked in tight. Blanket pulled up to my nose. I would secure myself as tightly as possible.

Initially, I thought I was just tossing and turning in the night. I was almost aggravated with myself because this was the only protection I had. This routine was the only thing that made me feel safe. And then it all went to hell. Up in smoke it went. *All* my security.

I awoke one night, and my covers were pulled down to the foot of my bed. I jumped up completely confused. I pulled them back over me. Extra blanket tucked over feet. Place additional pillow on feet because, yes, I must. Sides tucked in tight. Blanket pulled up to my nose.

Then it started happening at random. Some nights I would awaken and the blankets were pulled down. Other nights I would be fine. Now, whatever was in my room was having fun with me. It was like a freaking joke on me! The torment grew worse by the month. The creaking in the stairway, the vomiting, the hands under the armpits, the squeezing, the blankets being pulled down. As if that weren't enough, I started waking up with my head at the foot of my bed. *How is this happening?* When I closed my eyes, my head would be at the headboard. Extra blanket tucked over feet. Additional pillow placed on my feet because I must. Sides tucked in tight. When I'd awaken, I'd be lying on top of my covers with my head facing the *foot of my bed*. Panicked, I would dart back toward the headboard and slide under the covers and lay there wondering what next.

At that point in my life, I was too far down crazy lane to speak about these events to my parents or any other authority figure. No one was going to believe a word I'd say. Adults never believe kids. That's the rule. And the demonic realm knows this all too well. I confided in some of my close friends, but they weren't experiencing anything like it. *Yet.* Sure, they had some bump-in-the-night stories, but I couldn't tell if they were real or embellished. Kids love to compete. There are rules in life, and the demonic realm knows this.

For months I had wondered how I was ending up turned the wrong way in my bed. I tried to cope the best I could by telling myself maybe it was one of my parents. Maybe I fell out of bed, and they put me back in it ... backward? But, who? Why would my mother or father torment my sleep that way? , I practically slept with one eye open. There's no way they could pull that off without my knowing it. It just didn't make any sense.

One night, the answer I had been searching for finally came to me. I wished it hadn't. I was awake. But this time, it was different. Something didn't feel right. In fact, I *felt* nothing. You probably don't really understand, so let me repeat myself. I felt ***nothing***! The bed that I had grown accustomed to feeling pressed against my body was no longer there. My feet were exposed, and I could feel the air moving over them. I was ... floating. My mind started racing. Something was wrong. I kept my eyes closed. This made me feel safe. I had nothing else to hold on to. *Play sleep! Play dead! Who could it be?* I was certain it wasn't my mother holding me up at the witching hour. Nor my father. He'd never been the affectionate type anyway. And there were no smells, no fabric against my skin, no recognizable body parts, and no breathing. Just someone, something, holding me. I was horrified at the thought of opening my eyes because I didn't want it to know I was awake. I opened my eyelids just enough to fake sleep but still see. It had to be quick. If I was going to do it, it had to be quick. Just a glance. So I peeked. And what did I see? I saw ... nothing. *You've got to be freaking kidding me! This just keeps getting better!* It was dark. I just saw *darkness.* Then I felt myself being lowered back to my bed. As soon as I hit my mattress, I opened my eyes wide. I lay there on my back, my eyes working their way around my bedroom. Nothing. There was nothing. Nobody was there.

I had my answer.

Location, Location, Location

Growing up, my Uncle Gerald was one of the coolest people on earth. I mean, he's still pretty cool, I just don't tell him, to keep from gassing his head up. But growing up, I wanted to be like him. Just, cool.

My uncle used to drive a '90s Dodge Shadow. He put some work into it: custom sunroof, chrome rims, candy-apple-red paint job, and a great sound system. It was so loud that you could literally hear him blocks away. This car was amazing, and, of course, I wanted one.

Uncle Gerald has always been in the restaurant business, at least as long as I've known him. One of my childhood jobs was working for him at a Pizza Hut Delivery store. Say what you want about Pizza Hut now, but back then—wow! The ability to create your own pizza with just the right ingredients and cooked just how you like it is the closest thing to heaven. He was the store manager, and I was often a recipient of free food when I stayed with him. He's always done well in the restaurant business. He knows it inside and out.

Years ago, he told me about opening a store and what it took to run one effectively. Opening a store is something on my bucket list. But I'll never forget an important lesson he taught me. He told me that nothing else matters, not your customer service, not your food, not your store layout, none of it matters if your location is bad. If people can't find your restaurant or it's very difficult to get in and out of your location or if the traffic isn't dense, you'll be out of business. Location matters. It's the same with demons.

I repeat, location matters.

Like many believers, I have been guilty of ascribing all manner of evil events to Satan. I started down this path as a child. While I didn't need the church to convince me Satan existed, it did provide an identity for what I was experiencing. This was reinforced by conversations I had with my dad, who was a big believer in the devil. Movies, cartoons, Halloween, children's books, they all ascribed evil events to Satan. I later learned that this is the case because Satan was the adversary in the garden working against God's creation, man. He confronted Jesus in the wilderness. He confronted the early church and sent a messenger to buffet the Apostle Paul. Satan is the great dragon and deceiver of the whole world who was attempting to stop the birth of Jesus (see Revelation 12:4-9). He is seen as the antagonist in the greatest cosmic story ever written. So it makes complete sense to think of Satan first when we think of evil. However, we shouldn't think *only* of Satan when dealing with evil.

As we saw in the previous chapter, Satan wasn't the only one who hated mankind. The *Book of Enoch* tells us God bound the leader of the fallen sons, Azazel, for corrupting the earth. Along with being bound, all sin was ascribed to him. This tells us that Satan isn't alone. Satan is not our *only* enemy. Satan also can't be in more than one place at a time. In fact, the only being that is omnipresent is God. This begs the questions: "Where are the evil spirits, or demons, located? And what are they doing?" Certainly, they can't be hiding out in caves, completely unbothered by the human race, just waiting for that great day of judgment. The Bible doesn't lead us to believe that's the case. In fact, the New Testament is littered with demonic confrontations even after the death of Christ. We have no reason to believe the demons suddenly became reclusive and gave up their fight against humanity. Unfortunately, because the Bible is now closed and God's Church has been established on earth, the concern with the demonic has taken a massive backseat in our lives as believers. We've forgotten that many things that take place in our world are driven by demonic influence. And all warfare is ultimately grounded in strategy and deception: two necessary ingredients to ensure victory. However, location is also fundamentally important in battle.

Back in 1997, while serving in the United States Air Force, I was deployed to Ahmad al-Jaber Air Base, Kuwait, under Operation Southern Watch. I was a command post specialist. While I had a hundred administrative duties, ranging from coordinating search and rescue activities to disseminating weather threats, I had a more pressing responsibility. I was responsible for performing many communication activities leading up to and during wartime situations, such as the execution and launch of military forces. To this day I still remember sitting in the command post, monitoring a no-fly zone and ensuring no aircraft, and more importantly, no surface-to-air missiles, entered the space. If one did, I would have to politely execute orders to *take care of* the situation. Thankfully, on my watch this never became a problem I had to address. Even though I was on the ground, I was able to monitor the airspace thanks to the airborne early warning and control (AEW&C) aircraft that monitored Kuwait and the surrounding areas, like Iraq. The information that I was fed on the ground also was sent to our other brothers in arms (Army, Navy, and Marine Corps personnel) who were deployed in the region. Each of us within the United States military had a specific role to carry out, all of us working in tandem, all responsible for securing specific domains by using our influence of power.

The supernatural realm as it relates to evil forces is no different than a military unit. Just as military forces maintain certain airspace and land, demons do the same thing on earth. The only difference is we can't see them. But that doesn't mean they don't exist or that they don't influence people or things. Once again, all we have to do is turn to Scripture to see how this plays out.

During the life of the prophet Daniel, he encountered a divine being in one of his visions while in Babylonian exile:

I lifted up my eyes and looked, and behold, a man clothed in linen, with a belt of fine gold from Uphaz around his waist. His body was like beryl, his face like the appearance of lightning, his eyes like flaming torches, his arms and legs like the gleam of burnished bronze, and the sound of his words like the sound of a multitude. (Daniel 10:5-6)

This "man" caused Daniel to tremble and essentially collapse from fear. This was no normal man. In fact, it wasn't a man at all, and Daniel knew he was an angelic being, which was the reason for Daniel's fear. We see something similar with John in the book of Revelation:

In his right hand he held seven stars, from his mouth came a sharp two-edged sword, and his face was like the sun shining in full strength. When I saw him, I fell at his feet as though dead. But he laid his right hand on me, saying, "Fear not, I am the first and the last ... (Revelation 1:16-17)

Mary, the mother of Jesus, also had an encounter with a divine being—the angel Gabriel—and was locked in fear:

But she was greatly troubled at the saying, and tried to discern what sort of greeting this might be. And the angel said to her, "Do not be afraid, Mary, for you have found favor with God." (Luke 1:29-30)

In fact, God's angels were often known to show up and strike fear into people's hearts.

And Zechariah was troubled when he saw him, and fear fell upon him. But the angel said to him, "Do not be afraid, Zechariah, for your prayer has been heard, and your wife Elizabeth will bear you a son, and you shall call his name John." (Luke 1:12–13)

But the angel said to the women, "Do not be afraid, for I know that you seek Jesus who was crucified." (Matthew 28:5)

Daniel's encounter was no different than many others we see in Scripture when people come face to face with one of God's divine creatures. They all recognized that seeing an angel of the Lord was no different than seeing God Himself. They were fully exposed to the awesome power of the supernatural, which left them prostrate. The only human who elicited the same type of response from people was Jesus (see Matthew 28:9, Luke 17:16, John 11:32). To see Jesus was to be fully exposed before God. When Daniel came face to face with an angel, this spiritual being communicated to Daniel that he had been held up by an enemy, one who attempted to stop him from visiting Daniel to answer his prayers:

Then he said to me, "Fear not, Daniel, for from the first day that you set your heart to understand and humbled yourself before your God, your words have been heard, and I have come because of your words. The prince of the kingdom of Persia withstood me twenty-one days, but Michael, one of the chief princes, came to help me, for I was left there with the kings of Persia ... (Daniel 10:12-13)

We need to take notice of the title *prince* in reference to the being that is called the "prince of the kingdom of Persia." It may seem like this refers to a regular human being, however, that doesn't make sense within the context of the Scriptures. Not only was this spiritual being held up by the prince, but Michael, who is an archangel and is described as one of the chief princes, had to come to his aid. That is evidence that we're dealing with spiritual and not earthly beings. Also, if we look back at verse 12, we see this "man" came to bring Daniel a prophetic word because God has heard his prayers. So we know this was a messenger of God who was sent to Daniel. Their encounter becomes more intense as Daniel becomes mute and needs his mouth to be touched in order to speak. When Daniel finally responds, it's to question how he, a servant, can speak since his strength and breath have left him while in the presence of the visitor (see Daniel 10:16-17).

Lastly, this event is similar to one of Daniel's earlier encounters with Gabriel, another archangel. Gabriel had visited him to deliver insight and understanding while he was repenting for Israel's sins:

While I was speaking and praying, confessing my sin and the sin of my people Israel, and presenting my plea before the Lord my God for the holy hill of my God, while I was speaking in prayer, the man Gabriel, whom I had seen in the vision at the first, came to me in swift flight at the time of the evening sacrifice. He made me understand, speaking with me and saying, "O Daniel, I have now come out to give you insight and understanding. At the beginning of your pleas for mercy a word went out, and I have come to tell it to you, for you are greatly loved. Therefore consider the word and understand the vision. (Daniel 9:20–23)

Nothing about Daniel's situation was natural. It was 100 percent *super*-natural. And the prince of Persia was a formidable foe. In fact, so much so that Michael the archangel, one of the chief princes, had to provide support, so Daniel could keep receiving revelations from God. Just let that sink in for a minute!

Now, this prince of Persia isn't identified by name but by geographic location. And he clearly had some governing authority over Persia. Oftentimes, when we think about the spiritual realm, we tend to think of heavenly beings flying around completely detached from the earth and only concerned with humans who *inhabit* the earth. This may seem like a nuance that isn't important, but it's actually incredibly important. As we see, the antagonist in the story of Daniel has dominion over the land of Persia. He is referred to as the *prince* of the land.

The tenth chapter of Daniel introduces us to the third-year reign of Cyrus, king of Persia. Cyrus was responsible for allowing the Jews to return to Jerusalem. However, Scripture also tells us there was a great conflict. This great conflict was the playing out of the prophetic curse Moses spoke about in Deuteronomy 28 in which Israel entered the promised land and turned from God. Daniel was living during this apocalyptic time. Jeremiah warned that this prophecy was going to pass, and Daniel leaned on Jeremiah's prophetic writings (see Daniel 9:1) to gain understanding of his present situation. The events that were taking place in his day would ultimately lead to the fall of the Jewish people. Greece would eventually conquer the Persians, and Rome would one day dominate Greece. Behind all of this were evil forces ushering in this prophecy. If we look at Daniel 10:20, we can see evidence of this spiritual battle taking place:

Then he said, "Do you know why I have come to you? But now I will return to fight against the prince of Persia; and when I go out, behold, the prince of Greece will come. But I will tell you what is inscribed in the book of truth: there is none who contends by my side against these except Michael, your prince. (Daniel 10:20-21)

This is truly remarkable. The angelic being that was sent as a messenger to Daniel is going to return to Persia to fight against the prince of Persia. He also drops some futuristic knowledge on Daniel, letting him know that next up is Greece. And this is precisely what history records. Greece overtook the Persian Empire. What we deduce from this is that the fall of Persia was in fact part of God's apocalyptic plan, and demonic forces were fighting against this plan. Daniel's messenger, who was also fighting in this battle, had future knowledge of God's plan. And Michael, also referred to as a prince, is identified as the only one contending with this messenger.

We need to take special note of the term *prince* once again. Daniel's messenger didn't appear to have this title. So we know not every divine being is considered a prince. This title communicates authority, leadership, and hierarchy. We see this term not only given to heavenly beings like Michael and Gabriel, but also demonic ones like the prince of Persia. A very familiar verse that carries this title is in Paul's letter to the Ephesians:

... you once walked, following the course of this world, following the prince of the power of the air, the spirit that is now at work in the sons of disobedience ... (Ephesians 2:2)

The prince of the power of the air is believed to be Satan. Even he has been assigned this title, which speaks to his leadership and authority. In this verse, Satan's dominion is said to be the air, which clearly means he operates globally at any point in time. However, he is not omnipresent. This prince moves throughout the earth effecting change as a spirit of rebellion and disobedience. But who are the "sons of disobedience"? Are they humans or demons?

We need to remember there's history behind the demonic realm. The sons of God (Genesis 6) are the divine beings that rebelled, leaving their natural domain, and they took the women of mankind. These beings are bound within the earth (Jude 1:6). The spirits of the children born to the women who cohabitated with these fallen sons now inhabit the earth. It is these same rebellious, demonic spirits that Paul is referring to in Ephesians 2. Paul gives praise to God that he and the believers in Ephesus are no longer operating by the same spirit:

... among whom we all once lived in the passions of our flesh, carrying out the desires of the body and the mind, and were by nature children of wrath, like the rest of mankind. But God, being rich in mercy, because of the great love with which he loved us, even when we were dead in our trespasses, made us alive together with Christ—by grace you have been saved—and raised us up with him and seated us with him in the heavenly places in Christ Jesus ... (Ephesians 2:3-6)

None of this should surprise us. In fact, we can see the activity of supernatural powers tied to geography starting with the fall in the garden. It is here that Satan—who was established as a guardian over Eden—tempted Adam and Eve to rebel. This led to Adam and Eve being displaced from the garden. Another hostile territorial takeover happened when the fallen sons of God corrupted the entire earth, leaving God to cleanse it with a flood. We see supernatural activity yet again in the life of Moses, as God worked against Egypt for the purposes of setting Israel free so they could obtain the future promised land. We see more supernatural activity concerning geography when God fought alongside Israel to defeat every enemy to obtain the promised land.

Land is incredibly important. Location is incredibly important. Remember, God gave man dominion over the earth. The evil spirits that inhabit the earth are territorial and don't like that. They operate at a much larger scale than most believers realize. With evil spirits, everything is intentional. They don't just blindly wander into abandoned buildings out of sheer boredom.

If evil spirits are in a location, then there is a reason for it. This is vital for us to understand. Just as in combat, location can deliver victory or defeat. The right location can give way to victory. The evil spirits in the world aren't haphazardly choosing random places to hang out in. In fact, I am thoroughly convinced they are strategically placed at the command of their princes (leaders) around the world in anticipation of the end times. We know Jesus is coming back with an army of angels to wage war. We also know it doesn't take an army of angels to wipe out measly, sinful human beings, so clearly we're living in a period before the final angelic war, which we see in John's revelation:

Then I saw heaven opened, and behold, a white horse! The one sitting on it is called Faithful and True, and in righteousness he judges and makes war. His eyes are like a flame of fire, and on his head are diadems, and he has a name written that no one knows but himself. He is clothed in a robe dipped in blood, and the name by which he is called is The Word of God. And the armies of heaven, arrayed in fine linen, white and pure, were following him on white horses. From his mouth comes a sharp sword with which to strike down the nations, and he will rule them with a rod of iron. He will tread the winepress of the fury of the wrath of God the Almighty. On his robe and on his thigh he has a name written, King of kings and Lord of lords. (Revelation 19:11-16)

Make no mistake, this war is a territorial war. The end game is to usher as many people as possible away from God. But Jesus is coming to establish His kingdom. He is coming to wage war and execute judgment on believers and unbelievers alike *(see Revelation 20:12)*. He is coming to reclaim the entire earth out of the hands of those who have taken over.

Chapter Six

Man with Yellow Eyes

SHE WAS BEET RED. It looked as if she had been crying. My first thought was perhaps someone had picked on her. It was common for some of the other kids in school to harass her, because she was a little overweight. Kids can be mean, especially in middle school. But this day, Jenna seemed overly upset. In fact, when I walked up to her, she looked at me like she was broken. It was weird, almost uncomfortable. Jenna and I weren't terribly close, but we got along well. I was one of the few kids that didn't pick on her because I got picked on plenty. I attended a predominantly white school, and I was black and wore glasses. However, it was still unnerving when she walked up to me and gave me this look like she needed to be consoled and didn't care what anyone thought about it. She truly looked *shaken*.

I asked Jenna what was bothering her. Her explanation shook me as well. See, Jenna had introduced me and some of my friends to her Ouija board a while back. Through tears Jenna explained to me that she had put her Ouija board up before bed, but when she woke up in the middle of the night, the board was back on her bed. So she put it back in the box, placed it under her bed, and went back to sleep, thinking maybe she forgot to actually put it up. About an hour later she woke up again, and the game was lying back on her bed. This terrified her, so she took the game downstairs and put it in the trash. When she woke up in the morning, the game was back on her bed. Jenna put it back in the trash and took it outside to the detached garage that morning. She confided in her dad about what had happened, but he didn't have an explanation for her. She claimed her parents had nothing to do with it.

Standing there in front of her, looking at her red, glossy eyes, I was at a crossroad. My first instinct was to think she was making it up for attention. Despite having my own demons to worry about, for a split second I doubted her. I thought maybe this was an attention grab, but why? Why the Ouija board? Jenna wasn't necessarily a pushover, nor had she ever before acted out to get attention. Why did she look like a zombie? If it wasn't for her curly hair and pudgy cheeks, I really wouldn't have recognized her. She said I was the only person she had told. In fact, throughout the rest of the day, not one person came up to me to talk about Jenna and her Ouija board story. In that moment of listening to her account, while my mind raced to find a reason to doubt her, I realized the real impetus behind my seeking a flaw in her story. If her account was true, then everything I was experiencing could be true as well.

Sure, I had told myself my experiences were real. I was convinced they were real because of the obvious evidence; however, it was still only *my* experience. A part of me was holding on to the hope that it would all go away. That it wouldn't last. That I was just hallucinating. There was no one to corroborate my story so I could know objectively that the events I was encountering were true. Now, here I was, face to face with someone I knew, who looked like they were two breaths away from giving up the ghost, and I was shook. I didn't even know what to say to her except, "Really! What? Wow! Are you ok?" I mean, what else is there to say? The bell rang, and we both headed to our classrooms.

I saw Jenna later that afternoon, and she was still scared but much better. The next day I ran into her and asked how she was doing. She was doing well. No creepy events. No monsters in the closet. The Ouija board was gone, and she told me she was never messing with one again. Who knows, maybe her parents played a trick on her. If they did, it was beyond cruel, and there was no way anyone got sleep in her house that night. They would've been up all night waiting for an opportunity to pull the game back out to terrorize her, which didn't seem plausible.

As far as I know that was the only time Jenna had experienced anything supernatural. I never heard any stories from her after that day. It seemed nothing else took place in her house after that night. If it did, she kept it all to herself, much as I had been doing.

Here I was, still in elementary school, and I had become thoroughly convinced that my eyes and ears were not deceiving me. Evil was real and without a doubt there was something evil inside my home. And now, for the first time, it was beginning to look like I was not alone.

The Window

Tap, tap, tap. It was around three in the morning, and a noise woke me. *Tap, tap, tap, tap.* There it was again. It took me a second to realize it was coming from my window and not from somewhere inside my room. My brain had a hard time registering the tapping on my window. Something wasn't right.

Most of the Plattsburgh base townhomes were four, single-family structures. Each home had a detached garage several feet from the front of the home. All the townhomes were two stories, and all the bedrooms were located on the second floor. My bedroom faced the front of the house. My parents' and sister's bedrooms faced the rear. There were no ledges, eaves, or anything else that you could brace yourself on to reach a window. You needed a ten-foot ladder just to reach the second-floor windows. We did not have any trees or anything that could touch the outside of the house. I imagine this was according to the military housing code. So you can imagine my disbelief when I awoke to tapping on my window.

But this tapping wasn't some random, rhythmic noise hitting my window. It was deliberate, loud, and forceful. *Tap, tap, tap.* Then a pause. *Tap, tap, tap, tap!*

It was the same sound you'd hear if someone who knew you were home was knocking on your door and trying to get your attention. I was terrified. I sat up and just stared at those thin, blue curtains that separated me from whatever horrific sight was behind them. I couldn't fully make out the object that was outside my window. The streetlight produced enough light to help me see there was something dark swaying outside. I tried to think of what it could be. Maybe it was a person playing tricks on me. Perhaps it was a tree branch blowing in front of my window. Maybe it was a bird or a lost bat? But nothing seemed like a rational explanation. *Tap, tap, tap, tap, tap ... tap!* I was tempted to pull back the curtain, but I was too scared. Something told me to stay away from the window. I pulled the sheets over my head, eyes still wide open, and stayed still. Then it just stopped. No more tapping. I slowly pulled the sheets back and looked at the window. The shadow was gone. What seemed like an eternity of horror had lasted about ten minutes. Even though the tapping had stopped, I was too afraid to get up and look out the window. It took me about an hour to go back to sleep. I tried to convince myself there was a reasonable explanation for what happened for *all* the supernatural experiences that took place inside my home. The tapping was new, but surely it couldn't be real. So I thought.

The next day at school I ran into one of the kids who lived a couple houses over from me. We lived in the same building. He was a few years younger than me, so even though he lived a couple doors down we didn't really hang out. He seemed nice, though. I was having a pretty good day until he sprung his question on me. "Did you hear something tapping on your window about three o'clock in the morning last night?" he asked. I was shocked. How did he hear the same thing at the same time? This couldn't be possible. But clearly it was. I told him I heard the tapping and asked him if he went to the window to check it out. "No way," he replied. "I was too scared!" I told him I hadn't gone to the window either.

Neither of us had dared to look out the window. I was hoping that he had been braver than me, so he could tell me what was tapping. While I was relieved on one hand that someone else experienced this event, I was also frustrated and disappointed because I had *no* answers. *What was behind the tapping?* I felt like if I knew, it would somehow make things easier. It seemed like this answer was the key to unlocking one of earth's greatest mysteries. If I just knew what it was, I could better face it. For the rest of my time in Plattsburgh, I didn't get an answer to my question. I accepted the fact that I would never find out. That is, until decades later when my younger sister and I were talking about our time in New York.

My sister, Natalie, is five years younger than me. I kept a lot of the scary story stuff away from her because of her age, but also because I didn't really think she'd believe or understand. She was almost two when we moved to Plattsburgh Air Force Base. So, for the first few years of my hell, there was no reasoning with her. She was simply too young. But when I was in my thirties, I decided to give her a call to check on her. After some usual chitchat about current life situations, our conversation pivoted to our childhood and the crazy things we experienced. I shared with her that I had come across an article online that listed Plattsburgh as one of the most haunted cities in the country. In fact, unbeknownst to me up until that point, Plattsburgh A.F.B. was considered one of the military's most haunted bases before it was decommissioned. That's when she hit me with, "I believe it. Remember the man with yellow eyes?"

"Man with yellow eyes? No, I don't remember that," I replied.

"What? Yes. You don't remember when I told you about the man in my window?" she blurted.

I was beyond intrigued. I dealt with so much as a kid that this incident had clearly slipped my mind. I didn't remember that ever happening. I was blown away that she had experienced a supernatural phenomenon of her own.

"No, I don't remember that at all."

"Yeah, so you and I went to bed one night. I remember mom and dad were downstairs watching television. Then I heard someone tapping on my window like they were trying to get in."

"What!?" I yelped.

At this point I'm in freak-out mode. She continues with her story.

"Uh, huh. It was loud, so I got up to see what was outside my window. There was this man with yellow eyes staring back at me. It scared me, so I flung the curtain back and jumped into the bed under the covers."

I was floored. She also had had someone tapping on her window. I was stunned that she looked outside. Clearly, she was much braver than I was. I wish I had had that information when I was a kid because I needed backup. But this was the information I wanted. I needed to know what it looked like.

"So what did it look like? What did you see?"

"I just saw a black figure, a shadow with yellow eyes. All I could see were the eyes. I jumped in the bed and started crying."

I couldn't believe she was telling me this. All that time I thought I was the only one who experienced demonic activity. Not in a million years would I have guessed my little sister received her own dose of this disgusting medicine. As a big brother, I was also a bit angry that she never told me. Perhaps I would have been a bit braver—a bit more mad than scared, a bit more confrontational than submissive. Life oftentimes isn't fair. This was one of those moments. There were no do-overs, no second chances. I lost every round as a kid. But as an adult, I finally had my confirmation.

When you encounter a supernatural event, it's easy to dismiss it as a figment of your imagination. It's easy to pass it off as some random natural event with a rational explanation. You know, science and all. But what I learned that day was the confirmation I needed. Now I knew I was not alone. There were other people in the world just like me that were being exposed to the same types of horrors I was experiencing. They just weren't saying anything. And why would they? Who would believe them? You can't run these random events of supernatural phenomena through a scientific experiment. Demons don't exactly respond to orders or instruction.

Today, there is simply no way I can excuse away or ignore what happened to me as a child. Not only did I physically experience the forces of evil, so did other people in my life—on occasion, the same exact events at the same exact time in different locations. I've simply lived through way too much horror to be able to shrug it all off. And believe me, I've tried. My very logical and rational mind has looked for every loophole possible. But once—through God's sovereignty—other people in your life confirm *your* experiences, it's impossible to simply ignore them. After seven long years of hell in my old home, I am *beyond* convinced there is a very real darkness in the clouds.

Discernment

See to it that no one takes you captive by philosophy and empty deceit, according to human tradition, according to the elemental spirits of the world, and not according to Christ. (Colossians 2:8)

As followers of Christ, we often hear the term "spiritual discernment." Spiritual discernment is something most believers are taught to recognize as a gift from God. The sinner—now saved in Christ—is endowed with the spirit of God and now possesses the ability to exercise discernment. But discernment concerning what? I often feel as if this is another one of those "Christian" terms that is used without an understanding of its purpose. We all tend to talk about exercising discernment, but all one has to do is look at the fractured Church—especially in America. Every believer will tell you they have the gift of discernment—even the heretics.

I'm often taken aback by the discontent of people in such a rich country. I'm shocked at the amount of content we consume at the enemy's table, the time we waste in idleness, the lack of concern for our persecuted brethren, the airing of our church's dirty laundry to an already skeptical world, the ethnic division within our local churches across the country, and many other issues plaguing us believers. And these aren't even hard or complex issues, yet we struggle to discern that our enemy isn't other believers but the demonic forces that surround and manipulate us into apathy and disunity. Don't get me wrong. We are also at fault. I'm not of the ilk who claim everything is the devil's fault or that he *makes us* do it.

Humans can suck. We sin. A lot. And we should be held accountable for it. The truth is many of us struggle with practicing discernment. But, in order to be better at it, we must know what it means.

So what is discernment? Spiritual discernment, in its simplest definition, *is the ability to perceive things for what they truly are.* I want to stress something here. There is only *one* type of discernment. I believe this is an incredibly important concept to grasp. What I mean by this is that there isn't a *secular* type of discernment. Sure, the dictionary will give a definition about exercising judgment in a discriminatory manner for the purposes of gaining understanding. Then as believers we tack on the word *spiritual* to draw some sort of distinction or nuance because, well, we're Christians and we operate in the spirit. That distinction isn't necessary, though, for there is only one way to discern truth and exercise correct judgment for all things within the world, because truth comes from God as God *is* truth. You simply can't rob God of His own attribute as if truth can exist apart from Him. Discernment is seeing things through one lens: God's. It is seeing and understanding what is true.

Now, with a more practical understanding of the term discernment, let's look at the broader implications: "See to it that no one takes you captive by philosophy and empty deceit, according to human tradition, according to the elemental spirits of the world, and not according to Christ" (Colossians 2:8). Here the apostle Paul delivers instruction to the church in Colossae to deter them from accepting false teaching. What's interesting about his instruction are the realms Paul explicitly references—the physical and the spiritual—as well as the concern of being taken captive. Paul makes it clear that it is possible for believers to be persuaded away from the truth of God by human philosophy and deception, but he doesn't stop there. He also points out there are, what he calls, "elemental" spirits of the world that also perpetuate falsehoods based on philosophy and deception. Paul draws a distinction between what is human and the spirits of the world. He doesn't mince words or talk in code. Paul explicitly points out that for the believer there are spirits still bound to this earth that actively seek to ensnare them.

This is one of those moments that even now, as I write this, I wish I could fully express the angst in my heart as to why we must *get this*. I wish I could fully express just how much I want you and *every* believer to recognize the war in which we are involved. In the days of ancient Israel, Moses knew this when he saw God mock the gods of ancient Egypt by sending frogs, darkening the sun, turning the Nile to blood, and killing the firstborn sons and livestock. This was a direct, spiritual attack on the gods of Pharaoh, who were nothing more than demons posing as divine beings. The disciples also knew of this war as they walked with Christ, watching Him supernaturally manipulate creation while casting out demons. The early church fathers were also spiritually cognizant of this fact. Our enemy is not our fellow man but the demons who seek to lead every human on the planet away from God. And it takes discernment to recognize this affront on each and every one of us. A big difference between believers and those who are still lost is that believers are much closer to recognizing the truth of what is really transpiring within our universe. Demons know this and have made it their business to go all out to keep us deceived so they can continue to operate unnoticed.

Isn't it odd that today we don't *see* the level of demonic activity that we read about in Scripture? Think about this. Ask yourself what event transpired that caused all demons to pack up their bags and go home? And before you say the death and resurrection of Christ, remember that Paul and other apostles were casting out demons after Christ died, rose, and ascended. If you said, "nothing," you'd be absolutely correct. There has been no event. There is nothing in Scripture that tells us the demons took a vacation or decided no longer to plague humanity. But something surely has changed. So what is it?

This is where many people may try to argue science, science, science! That we're more civilized and have the advantage of modern technologies to put to bed the idea of the supernatural. But this demeans the ancient peoples who came before us as if they somehow were a bunch of ignorant goatherds. What of the ancient Egyptians? Do we strip them of their contributions to mathematics, writing (by way of hieroglyphics), and medicine, which relied on the scientific method? A method they invented! What of the Mesopotamian peoples who contributed to metallurgy, architecture, astronomy, mathematics (the value of Pi), and irrigation systems? What of the Aztecs and Mayans? Do we need to discuss the ancient Greek and Roman contributions to the world? It is terribly disingenuous and arrogant to think the civilizations of today are somehow more intelligent or advanced than those who had absolutely nothing to work with and no real previous foundations before them to build upon. The level of ingenuity they used to build their civilizations from nothing isn't anything to scoff at. Today's comforts are indebted to yesterday's discomforts. The brilliant minds of the past also believed in the supernatural, and that speaks volumes. I'd argue that if anyone is out of touch with reality it is, in fact, those who live within a modern society. Blinded by our technology, our senses are dulled by our comforts.

We also can't ignore recorded events, such as the casting out of demons where people—fully possessed by spiritual evil—were freed from their captors by Christ and followers of Christ. If we were merely talking about mental illness, that wouldn't explain how or why possessed individuals were able to return to their normal selves after the casting out of demons. There were no prescription pills or therapy sessions to attend. If these accounts weren't valid, then what we call exorcisms in our day would have failed, and we simply don't have any evidence that supports failed exorcisms. In fact, the only biblical account we have of a failed *attempt* was when the disciples were unable to cast an unclean spirit out of a boy in Matthew 17:16.

In this event, Jesus had to step in and help out the disciples for two reasons: One, they lacked the required faith necessary to cast out the demon (verse 20). Two, certain spirits require prayer as the instigation to an exorcism. We know this because of Mark's account:

And when he had entered the house, his disciples asked him privately, "Why could we not cast it out?" And he said to them, "This kind cannot be driven out by anything but prayer." (Mark 9:28–29)

This is an important thing to note. The disciples did not yet possess the necessary discernment to realize there were multiple ways to cast a demon out of a person. They did not yet realize that demons aren't created equal. Not all demons respond to simple vocal commands and the laying of hands. Not all demons affect their hosts the same way. In the story of the boy and the unclean spirit, the demon was referred to as a "deaf and dumb" spirit. It caused the boy to become mute and epileptic. Jesus expresses there are different *kinds* of spirits.

The chief reason why we fail to recognize the different kinds of spirits that affect humans in various ways is our lack of discernment. Our enemies have a massive advantage because they've existed for thousands of years. They know humanity better than humanity knows itself. So these spirits use this advantage of knowledge and time to carefully fit in and go unnoticed. Over time, and with each successive generation, these beings are slowly forgotten, unnoticed, flying under the radar, while fully operational.

Pivoting

When you think about it, there's a level of spiritual intelligence in operation that is uncanny. There's brilliance in the thinking of the demonic. This shouldn't be surprising. After all, these evil spirits are the offspring of the sons of God that fell. Scripture has made no claims that these spirits have disappeared into the ether never to be seen or heard from again. They've always been here. We're merely witnessing a change in tactics.

For most of my professional career I've spent a lot of time in and around tech startups. A term that I became very familiar with early on is *pivot*. To pivot means "to change direction." A pivot is typically what the founders of a startup will do when they begin to realize their current trajectory isn't hitting the mark. It is an attempt to change course, usually dramatically, in order to go after a better opportunity to avoid going out of business. This often means coming up with an entirely new product for people to consume. In the spiritual realm, we're not bearing witness to small adjustments in strategy but rather a full pivot.

Thousands of years ago, evil spirits were much more overt concerning their existence. Most—if not all—ancient peoples around the world worshipped some sort of god or goddess. This wasn't because they were searching for explanations behind the mechanics of the universe. No. It was because evil spirits were overt and active after God flooded the earth and killed the Nephilim. These spirits were and are dead set on peeling humanity away from God. In the ancient days we saw spirits posing as gods to draw people away from all things holy. Think of the Canaanites and Ammonites worshipping Moloch (also known as Kronos in North Africa). The Babylonians worshipped Marduk. We can't forget the ancient Egyptians and their many gods, or the Persian, Greek, and Roman religious practices. This just touches the surface. But the point is humanity has always worshipped the divine or what they've thought to be divine beings. The worshipping of supernatural beings by diverse peoples all over the world since the beginning of the human race isn't a coincidence.

I firmly believe that many people have the narrative *all* wrong. It's not that humanity somehow became confounded by the workings of the universe so that all peoples everywhere simultaneously invented their own deity. Then, as humans progressed in their intelligence and began to invent better technologies, we learned that the supernatural didn't exist. Why? Because now we can determine natural causations for the universe's operations. End narrative.

That is flat-out wrong. There's no evidence that ancient peoples invented deities due to lack of sufficient knowledge of how the universe works. That's a modern-day assumption that takes aim at theism. However, we *do* have evidence that ancient peoples—who spent a great deal of time discovering how the universe worked through what we call science—believed that their worship or lack of it could directly impact their livelihood. Remember, they believed in science and technology and were great inventors who paved the way for modern civilizations. Each civilization built upon the previous people's wealth of information and scientific knowledge. The argument that the supernatural was invented to fill the ignorance gap sounds more like a tactic from the demon's playbook. We can't have it both ways. Either the people living in the ancient days, who invented amazing technology and delivered massive contributions to the world, were grounded in science and wisdom, or they weren't. But they couldn't have been both profoundly stupid *and* incredibly intelligent. I think we owe them the benefit of the doubt.

The correct narrative—I believe—is that the supernatural has always existed and those living in the ancient days were exposed to their overt activities. This led to the worship of evil spirits, who were posing as divine gods. These gods—who possess supernatural abilities—were able to manipulate the natural world, to a degree, and provide insight only available to them. They used levels of trickery and deceit to convince humanity to worship them in exchange for well-being or the ability to *live your best life now*. And these demons had an amazing run, fooling the entire earth, so much so that God had to carve out a small set of people—Israel—to protect them from the demons' assault on humanity. Out of Israel we receive the Christ, Jesus, our Savior, who is God in the flesh. He arrived to reconcile humanity to God by His life's blood and to destroy the demonic strongholds laid upon the earth. This sends the demons back into hiding, because now they're exposed for who they truly are. But hiding doesn't mean they're defunct. It simply means these demons are operating covertly, behind the scenes. They had to pivot on how they assault humanity because their cover was blown.

Let me give you one important word: *war*. Remember we're living in a war. In war, you have to be strategic. The best example of this was when Jesus entered the scene and started confronting the entire demonic realm. The demons were forced to show their cards, utterly confused as to what was taking place before their eyes. Look at the story of the Gerasene demoniac and you'll see this play out:

And when he came to the other side, to the country of the Gadarenes, two demon-possessed men met him, coming out of the tombs, so fierce that no one could pass that way. And behold, they cried out, "What have you to do with us, O Son of God? Have you come here to torment us before the time?" (Matthew 8:28-29)

Just like the event with the possessed boy, Jesus showed up and the demons immediately recognized Him. However, they had no clue as to why He was there. They were so perplexed that they had to ask Him for a reason. The same thing happened when He delivered a man on the Sabbath.

And he went down to Capernaum, a city of Galilee. And he was teaching them on the Sabbath, and they were astonished at his teaching, for his word possessed authority. And in the synagogue there was a man who had the spirit of an unclean demon, and he cried out with a loud voice, "Ha! What have you to do with us, Jesus of Nazareth? Have you come to destroy us? I know who you are—the Holy One of God." (Luke 4:31-34)

You'd think that the demons would be fully aware that Jesus, the Son of God, was there to cast them out of people they'd possessed. But instead, they seemed rather confused as to why Jesus was there at all. It's as if they were expecting Him, but just at a later date and for a completely different reason. They knew they were destined for destruction, but the timetable didn't seem right to them, so they wanted to know why He was bothering them before the time of their demise. These demons had absolutely no idea that Jesus was on the earth to redeem humanity from right under their noses. Arrogantly, they thought the universe revolved around them. The fact that Jesus was on a rescue mission never crossed their minds. They understood this only after our Savior died and rose again. The withholding of this secret was revealed by Paul in his letter to the Corinthians:

Yet among the mature we do impart wisdom, although it is not a wisdom of this age or of the rulers of this age, who are doomed to pass away. But we impart a secret and hidden wisdom of God, which God decreed before the ages for our glory. None of the rulers of this age understood this, for if they had, they would not have crucified the Lord of glory. (1 Corinthians 2:6-8)

The entire demonic realm, including the fallen sons of God, believed they received the victory when Jesus was crucified. In actuality they took a certified L. This knowledge wasn't known to humanity but instead was a secret wisdom of God. If our spiritual enemies had known precisely why the Son of God was on earth, they would have done everything possible to keep Him from going to the cross.

Do you see why discernment is such a critical element to the life of a believer? Discernment is necessary in this war. The demons in Jesus' day lacked discernment and were unable to fully realize what was taking place because God kept certain knowledge *secret*. What the demons thought they saw transpiring was really an illusion. They held on to a false sense of victory. By the time they were able to see the truth, it was too late. Jesus had died and rose again. These same demons now await His return for the most epic of battles ever conceived. They know it leads to their destruction. However, they are committed to luring as many human beings away from God as they can so the destruction will be shared amongst God's special creation. They are now betting on the lack of discernment within the human race, which is compounded by our own pride and arrogance. Pride and arrogance? Yes! Just look at humanity today. There are two categories that people fall into as it concerns the demonic: **spiritual rejectionists** and **spiritual acceptors**. Both have fallen victim to hubris while these demons use a play from God's playbook: operate in *secret*.

Spiritual rejectionists flat out reject and deny any and all things spiritual. No theism, no spiritualism, no supernaturalism, only naturalism. Spiritual acceptors are willing to concede the idea that there are spiritual or supernatural forces at work, regardless of their religious bent. Sadly, neither position is safe from being duped by the demonic. Spiritual rejectionists chalk up every act of demonic activity to natural causes—even if the cause has no natural evidence to support it. Why? Because to them the supernatural can't be real. Demons have a field day with those who fall into this category. They don't even have to break a sweat to manipulate their lives. Spiritual rejectionists are easy prey. They're like wounded seals that killer whales toss around the ocean before finishing them off. In ancient days they most likely would have become believers of the supernatural, but, like many people today, they would have been lost as to what was truly of God. Their pride and idolization of humanity is their own undoing.

Spiritual acceptors are cut from many different cloths. They may or not be considered religious, subscribing to a main form of religion. It is possible they only refer to themselves as *spiritual*, not really worshipping any one particular deity. But they acknowledge that the supernatural realm exists. However, they are not safe either, as most spiritual acceptors believe nothing demonic or evil has ensnared them to any degree. Their belief in a higher power, divine spirit, or God has given them a false sense of security. The idea is this: *because one believes it to be, then it must be so.* But beliefs don't constitute truth. Something isn't true because one *believes* it to be true. Spiritual acceptors often deny that they, a family member, or a friend could be held captive by a demon. They're too spiritual for that to happen. The fear of speaking out and sounding like a lunatic is all the persuasion they need to allow the affliction to continue.

I've been following Christ for over twenty years and have sat under several different pastors. I can count on one hand how many of them have ever spoken about the demonic. I mean really spoken about it. And I get it. They don't want to sound like a lunatic or one of those overly charismatic, "name it and claim it," "fleecing the flock" pastors. What's next? Snake handling during service to prove Christ's power over Satan?

Because spiritual acceptors don't know how to properly walk this tightrope, the demonic holds power over them. Most don't possess enough discernment, and to top it off there's no instruction manual. So here we all are, grasping at straws and speaking in generalities about the demonic, but Christ and the apostles were always speaking in specifics. How is it that they recognized demonic activity and yet today as believers we're so inept? I believe tightly held traditions coupled with a false sense of security are the undoing of spiritual acceptors. Pride won't give us space to confess that most of us have *absolutely no clue* when it comes to the demonic realm. The demons not only know this, but I'd wager they expected this response after studying humanity for thousands of years.

All of this leaves us begging the question: *What can we do to turn the tables?*

Chapter Seven

Freedom

IT WAS 1990. I still remember when I received the news. I was torn but incredibly excited. My parents had received orders for our family. We were moving. Our new home would be RAF (Royal Air Force) Alconbury, England, which was an hour and a half north of London. Don't get me wrong. I didn't know anything about England, nor did I have the slightest desire to travel there, but it meant leaving our house. It meant leaving the room that had plagued me with horrors. It meant freedom!

To be fair, I actually liked living in northern New York. It was where I experienced *real* snow. Living in Plattsburgh meant lots of lake-effect snow, so blizzards were common. December always had the perfect Christmas vibe: snowboarding, sledding, snowball fights, all fun-filled freezing glory as a kid. Shoveling snow sucked, but it was a way to make quick money. S'mores around campfires, hiking up mountains, swimming in Lake Champlain, summer camp, and girl crushes are all stitched into my memories.

It was in New York that I learned how to ride a bike—without training wheels, mind you. My friends cheered me on, screaming for me to keep pedaling so I wouldn't die on the pavement. In New

York I learned how to roller skate and ride a pedal boat. I visited Niagara Falls. I saw my first WWF wrestling match in New York. The Ultimate Warrior was there! I remember trying my hardest to scream out of excitement, but I was recovering from laryngitis. Instead of roaring at the top of my lungs I sounded more like a balloon deflating. Oh, and how could I forget? I rode my first roller coaster at Great Escape. I had more firsts while living in New York than I can count.

I was certainly going to miss the few friends I had left. I say the *few* that I had left because many of my friends' parents had already received orders over the years and moved on. That's the life of a military brat. You don't really make a lot of friends, and when you finally make some, they eventually leave. And if they don't, you do. Yeah, it sucks. A whole lot.

But I was looking forward to moving to England. While I was sad, I was also relieved and curious as to what lay ahead. A large part of my curiosity centered on the evil I had experienced and wondering what it would be like in England. Would it be better? Worse? The same? All I knew for certain was that I wanted out of that room and out of that house. I had another question too. Would the next family that moved in endure the same evils? I'm not even sure there was a next family; the base was to be shut down in 1995 so families were being phased out over the next few years and stationed elsewhere in the world. Very soon, Plattsburgh Air Force Base would be no more.

Breath

The flight from New York to England was unbearable, but it was the first time in years I could sleep without fear. I wasn't used to sleeping peacefully. Even if I spent the night with a friend the fear of returning home was always looming. Fear is an odd thing. It keeps you on the tips of your toes. The nervous system is constantly in a fight-or-flight state. All senses are heightened. It is an enemy that becomes a close friend, and without it you start to feel alone, as if something is missing.

After living with it for years you feel almost exposed, like going out without your coat on a winter night. When lifelong fear becomes absent, you have to learn how to live without it. Now, on a plane with my worst nightmare being butt-chafed from the seating, I couldn't *really* sleep. Sure, I nodded off here and there, but I wasn't relaxed enough to sleep well. It *was* a seven-hour plane ride after all. However, England was waiting for me with outstretched arms, and I couldn't wait to get there.

When we arrived it was the same as usual. Base housing was full, so there was no availability. This meant we had to stay in billeting until something opened up. Eventually it did, and we moved into a house located off the base. Our new home reminded me of a cottage from a fairy tale. It was a two-story house with vines growing up it. It had a cobblestone exterior and no screens on the windows, which, as an American, I thought was beyond odd. The running joke was that you had to pay taxes on them if they were installed, so nobody owned window screens. However, this was most likely based on the fact that there indeed *was* a window tax in England—introduced in 1696 but repealed in 1851. The government in Britain loved their taxes. In fact, they went so far as to introduce a brick tax around the 1700s, but that was later repealed.

The house was nestled in a cul-de-sac, and directly behind it were plenty of trees. Behind the trees was an open field that had a walking path, so my sister and I used it to ride our bikes. This home had a fireplace with a hearth. The kitchen had stone floors which were burnt orange in color. Like our previous home in New York, it had three bedrooms. It was small, but nice. It was our new home.

I would be lying if I told you that I was completely relaxed in our cottage, that in my thrill and excitement of moving to England, I had somehow forgotten my past. No, I didn't forget it all. And while I was hopeful that things would be different in this new house, once I arrived that hope died. It wasn't even a slow death. There was no conversation between myself and my hope. No bartering, no discussion, no arguing, or debating. Hope killed itself right in front of me before I could speak any sense into it.

So there I was in our new home. On the outside I was smiling, but on the inside I was completely freaked out. I was terrified. I remember the first few days in the house I'd wake up in the middle of the night trying to discern the objects casting new shadows. After a week nothing happened, but I knew not to get my hopes up. It knew it was only a matter of time before the evil would show up.

A few more weeks went by, and nothing happened. I remember thinking to myself that the evil spirits might not know where I was … yet. Since they didn't know where I was, they might possibly be struggling to find me. But eventually they would, I just knew it. Evil spirits talk, and soon enough the evil spirits in England would show up. I just needed to give it some more time, I thought.

After two months I realized that the vomiting spells hadn't returned. I was surprised but confused. After three months I was in shock. *Could this be the end of it?* I thought. I had gone three months with no sickness, no evil visitations, not even a bump in the night. Every night, it was quiet.

It took me about six months to fully relax when I went to sleep at night. I was nervous that once I let my guard down the evil would return. I couldn't figure out why nothing was happening. Outside of the occasional sleep paralysis episode I was fine. *Did England not have evil spirits?* None of this made any sense. *Maybe the devil doesn't know I moved.*

In hindsight these questions sound a bit ... well, silly. But at the time I had no other explanation. And while I didn't know why nothing was happening, I did learn something important, a confirmation.

While living in New York and enduring the night horrors, I was convinced that *I* was the issue. At the time it seemed rather obvious that there was something about me that brought hell into my bedroom. I was so convinced that when I moved to England I expected the evil would follow me there. I figured the evil was attached to me so everywhere I was it would also be. While I have zero proof that what I'm about to tell you is absolutely true for every case, based on my own experience I believe there were two necessary components that allowed the attacks to gain a foothold in my childhood: location and calling.

Location

Living in a new location free from demonic oppression showed me that I wasn't crazy. It wasn't all in my head. The moment we moved to a new home it all stopped. Not slowly or begrudgingly. It was immediate. While living in New York I had received external confirmation from others around me, but there was always that nagging skepticism. Skepticism doesn't desire truth; it simply likes to rear its ugly head and make you question everything. Even today I am sometimes skeptical of what I clearly know to be the truth. But every single time it rears its ugly head, I'm met with undeniable confirmation of the truth.

The fact is most people won't encounter any kind of demonic activity in their own lives simply because they don't live in a demonically oppressed location. While it's true that my skin is black, you can also color me lucky, I guess.

Like most people, I had heard about haunted houses and buildings while growing up. The narrative usually consists of people dying a horrific death leaving their souls or spirits trapped on Earth. These souls supposedly wander hallways or corridors terrifying those who reside at the property.

I really hadn't given this narrative much thought until several years ago after I came across a creepy blog post. One day, I Googled Plattsburgh Air Force Base and hauntings. I don't even remember why or how I came to do it. However, I discovered a website containing archived stories of people living in Plattsburgh as a child. I read story after story about people who, like me, experienced traumatic things while living on the base. I also learned that the events weren't exclusive to the air base. People who lived off base also shared similar, supernatural experiences about the city of Plattsburgh. That's when I realized there was more to that place than I had originally thought.

Like all haunted places or things, there's a bit of a dark history behind Plattsburgh. The city sits at the center of a major U.S. victory from the War of 1812. On September 11, 1814, the British mounted an invasion heading south from the Canadian border with over ten thousand troops and a naval fleet in what is known as the Battle of Plattsburgh. They wanted to capture the city as it was the gateway to New York's main waterways. Despite being vastly outnumbered, the U.S. Navy, led by Master Commandant Thomas Macdonough, managed to secure a victory against the fleet of Royal Navy's Captain George Downie. It was a bloody and decisive battle that helped end the War of 1812.

Remember I mentioned that location is important. Wars are breeding grounds for demonic activity due to their very nature. Where such a conflict exists in which man—God's creation—is killing man, you can rest assured that demons are operating in full force. It becomes easy to assume that *only* humans are at the center of such egregious actions. While this may sound like a stretch, think back to the story of Daniel. The book of Daniel is very transparent concerning the underlying spiritual battle that was taking place at the time, as we saw the Prince of Persia resisting a divine being, sent by God to respond to Daniel. War is not foreign to demons. Their progenitors—the sons of God—are well aware of warfare:

And Azazel taught men to make swords, and knives, and shields, and breastplates, and made known to them the metals of the earth and the art of working them, and bracelets, and ornaments, and the use of antimony, and the beautifying of the eyelids, and all kinds of costly stones, and all colouring tinctures. (Book of Enoch, Ch. 8)[1]

What I find so interesting about the event laid out in the Book of Enoch is that it appears men were *not* initially versed in warfare. While sin entered the world due to Adam and Eve's transgression, humanity had not yet arrived at the point of warring against each other—at least not in any efficient manner. The sons of God changed that and even they realized location was important, as they attempted to subdue the entire earth after corrupting it. When Jesus arrived He reclaimed humanity through the shedding of His blood, defeating the demonic strongholds over man that existed. We now await the consummation of His work, bringing all things to complete fulfillment when He returns (see Revelation 11:15).

Location matters. Places of immense and bloody conflict are always ground zero for demonic oppression. Across the entire globe you can find story after story concerning spiritual activity in places of bloody conflict. Military installations are usually at the top of the list with bases such as Fort Leavenworth (Kansas), Kadena Air

---

1. The Book of Enoch, Sacred-Texts.com,
   https://www.sacred-texts.com/bib/boe/boe011.htm.

Base (Okinawa, Japan), Joint Base Pearl Harbor-Hickam (Oahu, Hawaii), and West Point Military Academy (New York) being prime examples. Then there are non-military installations such as Bhangarh Fort (Rajasthan, India), Salem, Massachusetts, the Tower of London (England), Alcatraz Penitentiary (San Francisco Bay), the Catacombs of Paris (France), the Langham Hotel (London, England), or the eerie Ancient Ram Inn (England). While these locations aren't known to have experienced bloody wars, they are known to be haunted due to their demonic or murderous associations.

For example, the Ram Inn is apparently home to an ancient pagan burial ground. Bhangarh Fort was supposedly cursed and the Archaeological Survey of India forbids anyone to enter the fort at night. Many people who ignored this rule committed suicide or died of unnatural causes while there. I obviously am not in the position to confirm or deny the supposed supernatural activity at these locations. If you search them yourself, you will often find some naysayers along with those who emphatically believe. That's because demons don't appear simply because someone wants them to. It's odd to me that people assume demons or "ghosts" should respond to them like a dog when called. I've read ridiculous stories about ghost hunters who bring Ouija boards and psychics to a location, only to leave disappointed because Casper the Friendly Ghost didn't want to come out and play. *Oh, the mockery! A demon decided not to show up! We brought paranormal equipment and everything! How dare they! They must not be real! We should scratch this place off of our list. Meh, science!*

I often laugh at this kind of fodder. It unfortunately displays an incredible amount of ignorance for the spiritual realm. Demons aren't our pets. They've got better things to do than to be summoned by some random fan.

Plattsburgh Air Force Base has had its fair share of paranormal "experts" conduct experiments too. Places that I grew up partly revering and partly being terrified of have been found by ghost hunters to give off paranormal vibes. The cemetery I referred to earlier is known to have spirits walking through it at night. The Old Gym was haunted by a soldier who roamed the building, and it was possible to see him even during the day. The old stone barracks were reportedly haunted. Even the flight line was supposedly haunted as airmen often reported seeing soldiers walking on the runway. I personally never saw any such apparitions in all the years I lived there, nor would I deny their existence. However, Plattsburgh is one location that evil spirits have decided to call home.

Most people won't have the unsettling pleasure of living in a location that is demonically oppressed. Therefore, they'll most likely never experience what seems to be fictional nonsense. This reality plays into the hands of the demons, giving them an advantage, as many people won't recognize their operations.

Calling

Location is the first thing that I believe can catapult someone into experiencing demonic oppression. However, it's not *always* necessary. There is something else that can drive demons to your doorstep, and that is God. No, not that God is sending demons our way, but by *calling* unto Himself, that attracts demonic activity.

I've heard it said that Satan isn't concerned with people living in sin—those hanging out in strip clubs, selling drugs, fornicating, and indulging in every possible fleshy desire. These individuals are already lost and have been claimed by the kingdom of darkness. This is the default position of every human being on the planet from birth. Everyone, from the moment of conception, is on a trajectory towards Hell unless God intervenes. It makes no sense for demons to randomly chase after people it already holds captive. Demons don't need to chase down people who are already headed towards them.

If we look at Scripture, we see numerous examples of either warnings or flat out attacks against those who belong to God. Much of this we've already covered.

One doesn't have to turn too many pages of the Bible to land on Genesis 3, which gives us the fall. Satan tempted Adam and Eve to dissuade them from what God commanded. And then there's Genesis 6 and the corruption of the human race by the sons of God. We can look at the assault on Job who was attacked in an attempt to get him to curse God and prove to God that man is a fraudulent creation. And what about Israel during the Old Testament days? God was constantly working through the Israelites, sometimes taking their lives in order to encourage others away from demonic, pagan worship.

In Luke 22:31 Jesus tells Peter that Satan was demanding to have Peter to sift him as wheat, most likely to see if he would deny or possibly curse Jesus, since Peter was such an emotional character.

We're all aware that Jesus was tempted by Satan, hoping He would fall and worship him. And we can't forget the disciples, who knew God's people were prone to spiritual assault, as Peter left us this warning: "Be sober-minded; be watchful. Your adversary the devil prowls around like a roaring lion, seeking someone to devour" (1 Peter 5:8). Peter wasn't speaking to nonbelievers. He was speaking to those who did believe. The Apostle Paul made it known a messenger of Satan was sent to harass him, but for a good purpose:

So to keep me from becoming conceited because of the surpassing greatness of the revelations, a thorn was given me in the flesh, a messenger of Satan to harass me, to keep me from becoming conceited. (2 Corinthians 12:7)

Scripture is replete with passages that make the message clear: *The demonic realm is only concerned with believers who are or will be a threat to their kingdom.* This is done in an effort to persuade humanity away from God. This demonic kingdom can achieve much more progress by going after high-profile Christians such as a pastor, than spending effort attempting to pick off individual believers who aren't a threat. If they can cause a leader or influencer to fall, then it can shake the faith of everyone who follows that person. The damage will be much more devastating and more widespread. It's a matter of scale and reach.

When I served in the military, I worked at the Command Post. This is a critical component to a base of operations, especially during war. It is from this location that the general and other high commanding officers communicate orders. Enemies know if they can take out this high-profile target, they can severely disrupt their military opponent. It would sever communications and leave troops in disarray. Without a general, the troops would be scrambling to establish order while under attack.

Spiritual warfare is no different. There are plenty of believers who signed up to serve, but most haven't actually been deployed to war, nor do they want to be. Most believers aren't actively engaging in warfare. And for them, much of what is believed to be spiritual warfare is nothing more than the flesh or simple life events unfolding in a fallen world. But for those who are actively pressing against the demonic realm by living as missionaries at home or abroad, spurred into deployment by God, they are undoubtedly on the enemy's radar.

Now, I want to take a moment to make one thing clear. I mentioned that Satan and the demonic realm aren't interested in those who are already lost. That is true. But it is true only in the sense that the demonic realm isn't concerned with capturing souls they already own. However, this doesn't mean those who are not saved can't be used, possessed, or manipulated for the purposes of advancing the kingdom of darkness. And oftentimes this is done without their awareness. We must remember this is war. No demon is conducting business mindlessly or simply for its own pleasure. *They have an agenda.* We just aren't privy to that information. This is another advantage they have over us.

All of this should serve as a warning to believers who are in the field of ministry. And ministry doesn't necessarily mean pastoral leadership. It can also mean serving the persecuted church, serving as a teacher of God's Word, engaging in street evangelism, or serving at any number of nonprofits to bring people the Gospel. There are different types of "ministries" that serve the Lord. There are also people who may not necessarily serve in a typical fashion, but they could be believers who have a tremendous amount of influence. Demons love to nudge such people into moral failures as an attempt to shine a light on the supposed hypocrisy perpetuated by the "self-righteous" Christian community. We see this in the story of Job. The world is eagerly looking for our downfall and we shouldn't be surprised. Satan—along with the fallen sons of God—made it his aim to show God humans aren't valuable. And those who reject the God of the Bible have the same spirit as the devil. So it makes perfect sense they, too, would seek to prove believers are not anything special. The sons of God say, "Those humans are nothing special. Watch and I'll prove it." The nonbeliever says, "Those Christians are nothing special. Watch and I'll prove it."

Location and calling. I firmly believe these are two critical underlying pieces that can act as catalysts for demonic oppression of a person, place, or thing. Sometimes only one is present, and other times both. They're not to be viewed as end goals but rather as means to an end. The question we need to ask ourselves whenever we detect demonic activity is: *What is the end goal?*

It's all too easy to become hyper-focused on the activity—which the demons are hoping for—and miss the forest for the trees. Distraction and subterfuge are tools of the enemy. As I sit here writing, I've been filled with frustration and disappointment by the response of many believers to the political climate during this time—there's so much hatred, anger, and derision towards one another. So many fleshly agendas masked in the cloaks of righteousness and justice. I have watched the demonic realm have a field day with the church—a body of believers that lacks enough discernment to notice they're standing in the middle of a war; a collection of God's children too ill-equipped to even know the first place to start to fight back; a Spirit-filled bride that would rather *be* the Groom, than to seek the Groom; God's tribe in the wilderness fed up with manna and screaming for meat at all costs; a people that would rather seek the philosophy and knowledge of men than drink from the fountain of God's wisdom—a fountain He offers freely and with great joy and pleasure.

Humanity, not Satan and his minions, has become our enemy. The wool has been pulled over our eyes. We should expect this behavior from the world, as they are lost apart from God. But the body of Christ should be the first to discern the real motives behind large-scale attacks. And while the world may not agree, as children in God's family, we simply can't afford to become untethered and rendered useless in this war.

Chapter Eight

Spirit over Flesh

You are in a war. If you remember nothing else from this book, know that you are in a war. I know I won't win the annual Positivity Award for making such a bold statement, but it needs to be said and internalized within every believer. When Jesus warned about the cost of discipleship, He wasn't playing around:

Now great crowds accompanied him, and he turned and said to them, "If anyone comes to me and does not hate his own father and mother and wife and children and brothers and sisters, yes, and even his own life, he cannot be my disciple. Whoever does not bear his own cross and come after me cannot be my disciple. For which of you, desiring to build a tower, does not first sit down and count the cost, whether he has enough to complete it? Otherwise, when he has laid a foundation and is not able to finish, all who see it begin to mock him, saying, 'This man began to build and was not able to finish.' Or what king, going out to encounter another king in war, will not sit down first and deliberate whether he is able with ten thousand to meet him who comes against him with twenty thousand? And if not, while the other is yet a great way off, he sends a delegation and asks for terms of peace. So therefore, any one of you who does not renounce all that he has cannot be my disciple." (Luke 14:25-33)

What do we really think Jesus is talking about here? Merely giving up some trite fleshly desires? To choose vegan versus keto? His words are literal, and there's an expectation to *literally* give up our own lives in order to pursue Him. Our conviction and readiness should propel us into the throes of death when required. If anyone needs convincing, Scripture doesn't disappoint. Consider these passages:

Indeed, all who desire to live a godly life in Christ Jesus will be persecuted.... (2 Timothy 3:12)

Beloved, do not be surprised at the fiery trial when it comes upon you to test you, as though something strange were happening to you. But rejoice insofar as you share Christ's sufferings, that you may also rejoice and be glad when his glory is revealed. If you are insulted for the name of Christ, you are blessed, because the Spirit of glory and of God rests upon you. (1 Peter 4:12-14)

Blessed are you when people hate you and when they exclude you and revile you and spurn your name as evil, on account of the Son of Man! (Luke 6:22)

Blessed are those who are persecuted for righteousness' sake, for theirs is the kingdom of heaven. Blessed are you when others revile you and persecute you and utter all kinds of evil against you falsely on my account. Rejoice and be glad, for your reward is great in heaven, for so they persecuted the prophets who were before you. (Matthew 5:10-12)

Scripture is littered with passages that make it crystal clear: **our decision to follow Christ is a deadly one** (see *Matthew 5:44, John*

15:19, Romans 12:14, 1 Peter 3:17, 1 Peter 4:16, 1 Peter 4:19, 1 John 3:13). This decision should not be taken lightly.

Following Christ isn't for the faint of heart. Anyone who chooses to follow Him must understand the full scope of what they are entering into. Too many people step into this faith with a false expectation of life becoming easier, full of more material blessings because they now worship Christ. But God doesn't promise any of these things. From Genesis to Revelation, we see the people of God in a constant state of struggle with the world and spiritual forces. The Bible *is* clear that we can expect life to become much more difficult and at times filled with suffering for Christ's sake. If you are fortunate enough to live in a country that is democratic in nature and wealthy, it's easy to think life is supposed to be filled with material blessings: a well-paying job, great health, bustling business, a family with a picket fence, and a sizable investment portfolio waiting for you at retirement. We say, *look at God work!* But if you live in a country that is a dictatorship and are under persecution and kicked out of your village for your faith, most believers living in a wealthy country would dare not look at you and say, *look at God work!*

The truth is believers who are not living a comfortable life but are in hard places throughout the world are more in tune with the spiritual war that is taking place. Many are on the front lines of the battlefield each and every day. Not because they have some sort of persecution complex or they've committed an egregious sin or because God is angry with them. No! It's simply a result of God's sovereignty and His chosen geographical placement of those who are persecuted. Those who do not live under persecution are also recipients of God's sovereign placement. While we may all be equal in God's eyes, our missions may not be. But you can rest assured everyone has a mission.

Realizing the war is real and accepting your mission is the very hard part about being a follower of Christ. This is the part so many believers would rather not think about. When our Lord warned that there was a cost to being His disciple, this is what He was referring to. One must be willing to give up one's life, not just in death, but also in the pursuit of living.

To give up one's life in the pursuit of living is to be born a new creation with new desires and a completely different outlook on life. Jesus helped Nicodemus understand this after he came to Him in secret:

Jesus answered him, "Truly, truly, I say to you, unless one is born again he cannot see the kingdom of God." Nicodemus said to him, "How can a man be born when he is old? Can he enter a second time into his mother's womb and be born?" Jesus answered, "Truly, truly, I say to you, unless one is born of water and the Spirit, he cannot enter the kingdom of God. That which is born of the flesh is flesh, and that which is born of the Spirit is spirit. (John 3:3-6)

This exchange between Jesus and Nicodemus is perhaps one of the most overlooked yet one of the most powerful passages in the Bible. Sure, on the surface we see that Nicodemus is being made to understand the language of what it means to be born again. But look more closely and you'll see Jesus is drawing a clear dividing line between the kingdom of the world and the kingdom of God.

He is communicating that you can't even *see* this kingdom as one born of the flesh. This aligns with the exchange Jesus had with Peter who confessed Jesus was the Son of God: "And Jesus answered him, 'Blessed are you, Simon Bar-Jonah! For flesh and blood has not revealed this to you, but my Father who is in heaven'" (Matthew 16:17). What Jesus is getting at is there are literally two realms. One is spiritual and the other is earthly or what we'd call natural. It is only by way of being born again that we can even discern the spiritual world. Yes, *discern*. The spiritual world isn't incredibly easy to tap into, and, in fact, Jesus tells Peter that God had to reveal who Jesus was to Him. Realize that many people saw the same miracles Peter did and still rejected the Christ. So it is not a matter of understanding through the flesh. What we see is there's this sort of spiritual connectivity that takes place once God grabs hold of us and makes us children of the kingdom. And here's the thing: We aren't given a new purpose in life. We are merely made aware of the purpose God had already predestined for us.

This is akin to the butterfly, one of God's most amazing creations. Butterflies go through four stages. They start out as an egg, then go through a feeding stage which turns them into fat little caterpillars. They become a pupa in the third stage, and it's at this stage the butterfly begins its transition. This transition takes time, and it looks like nothing is actually happening. That is, until the butterfly emerges with a completely different look. They no longer inch their way along the dirt but now fly, giving them a new perspective on life from heights they couldn't previously have imagined. Once a muted caterpillar, they are now fully decorated with beautiful colors you could spot from a distance. The butterfly is nothing like the old creation. Post transition, its entire perspective on life changes, because it is truly a new creation with a completely different view— literally and figuratively.

So it is with the believer. Our entire perspective on life should be different after our transition from slaves of the enemy to slaves of Christ. When we look at the world, our lens should be sharper. Our view of the world should be different because we are now operating from a new height. We are no longer grinding, crawling, and inching through the dirt, tunneling through the earth's landscape with a very narrow view. As soldiers of Christ—as new creatures—we should be able to look down at the world and see the full picture. We can look back at what we once were. We can remember the struggle and the path taken to get where we currently are. We can praise the transition God put us through. We will be awestruck at the true realities of life instead of being duped by the false narratives we've been fed by the world. Know that if you are in Christ, *you are no longer of this world*. "But our citizenship is in heaven, and from it we await a Savior, the Lord Jesus Christ" (Philippians 3:20).

Here's my point. We simply don't have a choice or a say in the matter as it pertains to being stuck in this war. We are caught between two worlds, albeit we fight on the winning side. Demons don't care if we have decided not to engage in the war. Sideline believers still impact the game. Pawns on a chessboard still have usefulness. No one can hide from the war or render themselves useless. No one can afford not to be bothered. Because even if you are a believer that is not operating on a mission and pressing against the kingdom of darkness, you can still be manipulated into being rendered obsolete to the kingdom of God. Or your manipulation can lead to someone else's destruction to score points for the enemy. No one is safe. This is why Peter warned that we should be alert for *our* adversary is "seeking someone to devour" (1 Peter 5:8).

The goal of the entire demonic realm is to render every believer obsolete to the kingdom of God, all while challenging God's assertion that humans are special. Their aim is to separate humanity from God.

I pray that by now you realize you have signed up to fight against the kingdom of darkness the moment you affirmed your faith in Christ. There's no way out. I also pray that you realize that those who do *not* follow Christ aren't spared this war either.

Family

Take a serious moment for self-reflection. Why? Because it's incredibly easy to talk about spiritual warfare, Satan, demons, spirits, and evil while not recognizing the role we as humans play in all of this. We often abstract ourselves away from evil as if we're above it and live unscathed. When we talk about the spiritual realm, we usually speak as if there's a *them* and an *us*. It's easy to draw a line in the sand to distinguish our two realms.

But ask yourself, when you see evil in this world—murder, racism, marginalization, rape, sexual perversion, and more—do you view your fellow sinner as the one to defeat, or Satan? Do you find yourself angrier with humans than with the demonic realm? Where is your anger placed? Do you pray against the spiritual powers that operate unseen, or are the majority of your conflict prayers against men and women? When you wrestle with things of this world, are you quick to grab a book based on the philosophies of man or do you grab the Bible? If you have a collection of books, are they based on biblical truths or man's ideas for solving worldly problems?

This is important and it's hard. If we are honest with ourselves, we typically project our anger and frustrations upon those whom we can see: humans. We are ready to go to war with those with whom we can physically engage. It's easier to give another human a piece of our mind. Don't get me wrong, I'm not advocating that we ignore the sins of men. I'm advocating that we also hold the evil spirits responsible for instigating our corrupt world into the state that it is in. This doesn't mean humans aren't culpable for their sins. What it means is that we need to recognize the part our true enemy is playing.

If you read James, it's easy to believe humans can be our enemy:

You adulterous people! Do you not know that friendship with the world is enmity with God? Therefore whoever wishes to be a friend of the world makes himself an enemy of God. (James 4:4)

But Scripture doesn't encourage the idea of humanity being an enemy of humanity. James 4:4 tells us that people who reject God are enemies of God, not enemies of God's people. Here's a way we can better frame this.

Before you think of people as being your enemy, ask yourself, *who made you God?* This may sound a bit harsh, but *really* think about this question. Who are we? We are but dust created from the ground. We have no righteousness of our own. We possess no inherent goodness. Our objective moral code was received from God. We were so lost and destitute to the spiritual things of life that God Himself had to intervene to the point of sacrificing His own Son to reclaim us. We were dead and made alive and only by God's doing, not our own. The very people we hate are the very people we once were before God transformed us. Only God has the right to have enemies. We don't.

In fact, Jesus attempts to change the way we think concerning our "enemies" in the book of Matthew:

You have heard that it was said, "You shall love your neighbor and hate your enemy." But I say to you, Love your enemies and pray for those who persecute you.... (Matthew 5:43-44)

Jesus wasn't trying to encourage His followers to have enemies. In fact, He was doing the opposite. He spent time trying to rewire our understanding concerning who we call our enemies. Instead of hating or disparaging others, our Lord instructed us to love and pray for them. When Peter sliced off the ear of Malchus—the high priest—Jesus instructed Peter to put away his sword. Jesus then healed the ear of Malchus.

If we look at Proverbs, we see it instructs us to essentially exercise humility and grace towards the wicked:

Do not rejoice when your enemy falls, and let not your heart be glad when he stumbles, lest the Lord see it and be displeased, and turn away his anger from him. (Proverbs 24:17-18)

This is a hard pill to swallow for most of us. We typically like and desire when our enemies *get what they deserve*. We want to see God exercise justice. We want Him to dole out retribution while we enjoy the show. But Proverbs tells us that God can actually turn his anger away from our enemies because of our own pride. Again, we really need to remember who we are. God is just, not us. God is good, not us. God is holy and righteous, not us. All that we are—that is like Christ—has been imputed upon us by God. We don't own any of it. Proverbs is a reminder that we are all the same.

God wants us to remember we are all *one* human race. We are one *family*, who has been subjected to physical and spiritual corruption. And while people will always sin against us—at times in the most egregious ways—our true enemy is not our fellow man. Instead of warring against our human enemies, we should be praying for their eyes also to be opened to the spiritual wickedness they've fallen victim to. Man is not *our* enemy. Man, after pitting his heart against God, is *God's* enemy. But man is *not* the enemy of man. To believe differently is to play into our true enemy's hand.

The fallen sons of God know *they* are the real enemy. Satan knows *he* is the real enemy. The demons that operate within the world know *they* are the real enemy. They have all mastered the art of deceit. They have fooled the world into thinking they don't exist, or they aren't a factor, and that man is the true enemy.

Remember your enemy. It isn't your fellow humans.

The Goal of Spiritual War

War is ugly. It's costly and human blood is the currency. But war always has a purpose. The purpose may not always be obvious, and it may not always make sense, however, know that there is a purpose behind every war.

Adam and Eve may have disobeyed God, but it was the other race within our family that declared war on humanity. We'd do best to remember the correct narrative. The narrative of sinful humanity which has created an "us versus them" mentality is false. Even Jesus attempted to correct this false narrative. We are called to love our enemies. This is akin to loving our own family members regardless of how they offend us. And yes, it is hard. Very hard. It isn't a call to ignore the transgressions people commit. It doesn't mean we allow people to abuse and subjugate the weak. It certainly doesn't mean we shouldn't defend ourselves when violently attacked or that criminals shouldn't receive earthly justice. But it does mean love should still be at the very core of everything we do that involves humanity, whether that's defending ourselves or exercising justice. This is how God treats us. Everything He does is grounded in complete love.

But love isn't at the core of those who war against humanity. It is hatred. It is disgusting, vile, filthy, irrational hatred for you, your children, your parents, your friends, your pastor, your spouse, your brother, your sister, and anyone else that you know or ever will know. It is the kind of hatred that stirs up blind wrath. I've seen this very same wrath, and if you live long enough you will as well. It is a contagious sort of thing. It is the kind of wrath that pits an entire ethnic group of people against another almost to the point of extinction. It is the kind of wrath that sits at the center of world wars. It lusts for genocide and dines with persecution. And it makes a mockery of God's handiwork. If you haven't seen this kind of wrath, you've undoubtedly heard of it. It's the same wrath that led humans to joyfully nail their own Savior to a cross after stripping his flesh to the bone.

The propensity to sin and to hate resides within all of us. Scripture commands us to be angry but do not sin. Do not let the sun go down on our anger (Ephesians 4:26). The very next verse warns not to give any room to the devil. Do you see how this works? Our anger for one another can create an opportunity for the demonic realm to ensnare us. The fallen nature of each and every one of us makes this possible. Before we know it, we're exercising blind rage and are ready to kill. Once we are ready to kill, we are in position to do the devil's work. There is a reason—in fact several—as to why we are commanded to abstain from murdering one another. It's not simply because it isn't a nice thing to do. And there's a reason why we're called to address our anger before the sun goes down.

Anger is like the sea—it doesn't rest. It is powerful and in the right conditions creates waves that can destroy any ship. But it is always flowing. Anger likes to become hatred. It isn't content with being an infant. It wants to grow up into something larger and more powerful, so it evolves into hate. Once it becomes hate it no longer exhibits the characteristics of God. It has become something else. Hatred can't be reasoned with or talked down off the ledge. Hatred doesn't like debates. It likes quick and decisive action no matter how irrational. Hatred will cause us to murder. Murder will literally land us in hell.

In Matthew 5 Jesus talks about anger when addressing the sixth commandment, thou "shall not murder" (Exodus 20:13). He wants

His audience to know that they've completely missed the point. Before Jesus broke down this commandment, it was assumed that as long as you didn't murder anyone, you didn't break God's commandment. Jesus helps us to see that just being angry can cause us to be liable of judgment. Judgment is okay. But we need to tread carefully when we are angry because if we're found guilty of sinning while angry, then we'll be found guilty of breaking this commandment. Jesus goes even further and states that if you call your brother a *fool*, you're liable "to the hell of fire" (Matthew 5:22). We are called to go to our brother or sister and make amends before it's too late. It is important to note that Jesus was addressing the issue of the heart. Before we commit any action with our hands, we will first be motivated by what's in the heart. Sin is and has always been an issue of the heart. Our Savior is warning us about where our anger will take us if left unchecked or unresolved.

Hell isn't the only reason we're called to abstain from murdering. We're also called not to commit murder because we don't have the right to take innocent lives. This is like a school bully who has made it his prerogative to take everyone's lunch money. He knows he has nothing to do with the money in his own pocket, yet believes he has the right to steal everyone else's. But the taking of another's life is exponentially more serious than stealing lunch money. God is the creator and sustainer of all life. It is robbing someone of a gift given to them by God. It is playing God. It is an attempt to *be* God.

To be God is precisely what the fallen Sons of God and Satan desire. They woke up one day and chose anger based on jealousy of humanity. They were angry at what God did in creating humanity.

This fomented into hatred. This hatred became the necessary weapon for wiping out the human race. Whenever we choose hate we literally commit ourselves to the work of demons. We are doing their handiwork.

This spiritual war that we are all part of has been built on a solid foundation of deception and hate. And the goal, the final act for the demonic realm is to separate humanity from God. We must remember this whenever we find ourselves angry with one another. We must remember this when we see societies divided and humanity at war with itself. If our temporal goals for humanity cause eternal separation from our Creator, then that is a sure sign we are achieving the goals of the demonic realm.

Chapter Nine

Swords and Shields

As I sit here contemplating how I want to deliver this chapter, I'm met with the arduous task of shining a light on what can't be seen. This chapter is the most difficult to write. I so badly wish I could simply bottle what's swimming in the ether and deliver it in a very tangible manner to you. The demonic realm has done a great job at conflating very real, supernatural events with natural ones. And it doesn't help that the pride of man has slowly chiseled away his need for God, placing science—man's handiwork—upon the altar for worship. Then there's the church, which has sadly forgotten that it is in the middle of a war—a war for souls. All of this has left many believers blind to the realities of life. We truly need God to reveal to us what our flesh can't see.

There is so much that could be said about what I'm going to share. And so much that I won't be able to cover because it would prompt the need for another book. But hopefully I can kick-start a new way of thinking for you. That is the chief aim of this chapter, to help you change the way you view life to better recognize spiritual activity.

I want to do my best to leave you with wisdom so you can be a better soldier in this war. My hope is that if you have children, you can use this information to prepare them for the war too. The demonic realm doesn't discriminate, and children are the easiest prey because they are so naïve. I know this from experience.

Little Ones

Children's minds are so malleable. It is so easy to corrupt them, to seed propaganda. Everything is a fantasy to them. The world is nothing but one giant opportunity to live out their wildest dreams. Solomon commands parents to train them up in the way they should go (Proverbs 22:6). Because, left to their own devices, they will oppose God and seek their own way. This is the normal course for every human being on the planet (see Luke 18:19, Romans 3:11). And it makes sense because it's the *natural* way.

We need to guard our children. The enemy has long infiltrated television and the internet as well as public and private school systems. Many of us who have been blessed with children have traded away our guardianship for convenience and selfish ambitions. The desire to pull your children closer so you can train them up will cause people to demonize you. For example, I've seen our current society do this to the many who homeschool their children. The narrative is children should be socialized by other immature children because apparently children go to school for socialization not education. Apparently, children can't be socialized properly unless they're away from their guardians. Even the animal kingdom doesn't believe such a thing. But we've bought into this lie. Kids everywhere are sent away to public and private schools inside the mouths of lions to be "socialized" by those who have no desire for God. And the church has paid the price. However, I want to be sensitive to those who have no choice but to place their children in such school systems. It doesn't make parents bad or ungodly. My point is only to highlight society's tendency to berate believers for withdrawing from the world systems. Millions of believing parents are frustrated with school systems and organizations that teach the most godless of things. Instead of pulling our children out of the lions' den, we send them back while complaining about the den.

And what of the treatment towards the many mothers who live in our modern-day society? My country—the United States of America—shames mothers who choose not to enter the corporate world and pursue ladder climbing, and it doesn't stop there. Any husband who approves of his wife making this decision is also shamed and demonized as archaic, selfish, and controlling. It is feminism on overdrive. The reason for this behavior is obvious. It is *much* easier for the demonic realm to get to our children if we are distracted by work and no longer guarding them. So a very basic and primitive instinct such as caring for and training up your seed is frowned upon. Exercising your God-given duty is now deemed as harmful. It is no longer the first priority. It has become the last.

Parents, guard your children. We should know who they know and the beliefs of those in their circle of friends. Parents, *guard your children*. Know what they watch and what content they have access to. Literally *nothing* is safe anymore. This isn't a call to panic but a call to awareness and to the exercising of caution. Today we have children's television shows that introduce sexual perversion as being normal. As of the writing of this book, the average age a child will be introduced to porn is thirteen. Remember, that is an average. Some children have seen porn at *eight years of age.*

Fight the New Drug is a nonreligious and nonlegislative nonprofit that exists to provide individuals the opportunity to make an informed decision regarding pornography by raising awareness on its harmful effects using only science, facts, and personal accounts. Their website cites recent studies and the effects porn has on children:

Studies show that most young people are exposed to porn by age 13, and according to a nationally representative survey of U.S. teens, 84.4% of 14-18 year-old males and 57% of 14-18 year-old females have viewed pornography.[1]

To make matters worse, many elementary schools are teaching ideas such as transgenderism to children as young as five to encourage them to explore their own sexuality. I don't know what you were doing at the age of five, but I can tell you the exploration

---

1. "How Many People are on Porn Sites Right Now? (Hint: It's a Lot.)," Fight the New Drug, April 5, 2022, https://fightthenewdrug.org/by-the-numbers-see-how-many-people-are-watching-porn-today./ British Board of Film Classification. (2020). Young people, pornography & age-verification. BBFC. Retrieved from undefinedundefined. Wright, P. J., Paul, B., & Herbenick, D. (2021). Preliminary insights from a U.S. probability sample on adolescents' pornography exposure, media psychology, and sexual aggression. J. Health Commun., 1-8. doi:10.1080/10810730.2021.1887980.

of my sexuality was no match for my Hot Wheels cars, Legos, '80s cartoons, and Big Wheel.

People used to struggle with their identity as it relates to family or culture. Now humans have become confused as to what being human is. Society is becoming increasingly ill. The world is experiencing some sort of mental sickness where one's gender is now based on what one believes it to be. People are mutilating their God-created bodies in an attempt to change their biological sex. And this is being encouraged by the medical community. For example, the Mayo Clinic Health System advocates for children deciding to switch genders:

Remember that while their brain—not their parts—determines their gender, trans children still needs [sic] health care based on their anatomy, regardless of their gender identity or expression. This includes age-appropriate screenings and vaccinations.[2]

No longer are the terms *sex* and *gender* interchangeable. A hard line now exists as sex refers to biological anatomy while gender is exclusive to social roles. But these terms have been obfuscated to the point where if one thinks they're the opposite sex, then they must be. Yet, if I were to claim that I'm a seven-foot Asian man with blue eyes, people would think I was crazy. I'm Black with brown eyes and well short of seven feet tall. However, for some reason I

---

2. "Advocating for transgender children's health care," July 27, 2021, undefinedundefined hometown-health/featured-topic/advocating-for-transgender-childrens-health-care.

would be called mentally ill if I identified that way because of the obvious physical evidence. If someone claims they hear a second voice in their head, they're called mentally ill and are ascribed the condition of Schizophrenia. Yet, if a boy desires and believes he is a girl—regardless of the evidence—then his belief must be true, and it is normal.

With all of its supposed knowledge and worship of science, the world becomes an incredibly illogical, emotional place. When sin becomes its god, inconsistency reigns. And in our day it is the god of sex. While we as parents often love to think we've bolted every door shut, we need to remember the enemy is a master at picking locks. And thieves often show up when no one is around to catch them.

Hubris loves to make a mockery of parents. As someone who has spent twenty years working in tech, I promise you that even the "safe" applications and games supposedly suited for children aren't safe. Even educational and social media applications drug the children by rewarding specific behaviors. These reward systems for successfully accomplishing a task alter the chemistry of the brain, just like porn. Every reward earned sends dopamine rushing through the brain. And contrary to popular belief this all starts at infancy when parents buy as many loud and colorful toys as possible for their baby. We then wonder why children can no longer sit quietly, focus, and concentrate—or be left alone with their own thoughts. We've completely overlooked the effects of overstimulating our children. Parents are creating drug addicts without realizing it. This may sound a bit extreme. But as someone who has taught Sunday school classes with children who can't peel their mobile device away long enough to learn about Jesus, I assure you it's a very real problem—a problem that clearly isn't exclusive to nonbelieving families. Just visit a restaurant and you'll undoubtedly see disengaged children sucked into their devices like addicts.

Know this: God cares for His children. He cares so much that He took on flesh as Christ to die for each and every one of us. As parents we should be willing to sacrifice everything to guard our children.

Parents, guard your children like your life, no, like *their* life depends on it. Because it does.

Family Dynamics

If you live in America, then you're probably already aware that over 50 percent of Christian marriages fail. How did this happen? While I could speak to some of the more obvious causes that simply roll up to unequally yoked or immature spouses, I want to focus on the spiritual aspect of things. The not-so *obvious* things. Remember, shaming women into the workforce and not allowing them to spend time with their children has an impact on the family dynamic. And if this is not a representation of your family setup, don't think you're out of the woods yet. Remember, hubris is not our friend.

The entire human race rests against the backdrop of family. The same argument can be made for much of the animal kingdom as well. When God created the heavenly beings, he didn't do it out of necessity. However, a heavenly family was established and composed of different types of diving beings. When God created Adam, it wasn't out of necessity. Adam was brought into God's family, but

Adam was different. He was human. God, in His infinite wisdom, realized Adam needed a counterpart that was like him. This is where Eve comes in. She was created from Adam's rib. Adam and Eve were the first human family but were also part of God's family. God is a personal Creator being who desires relationship. God's human and divine creations need and desire relationship. Even those who reject God need and desire relationship. It's wired into our DNA.

Satan and the fallen sons of God desired to disrupt God's family. They got their wish, but their work isn't complete. The very righteous, holy, and perfect idea of family was destroyed well before you and I arrived on earth. That means our perspective on family has been marred by sin and corruption. Family is something we have to fight for. When we think of family, our thoughts should find their final destination at the gates of heaven. We not only should have our human family in mind but also our divine family. We should have God in mind. And to be fair, the evil ones that have been kicked out of God's family were originally part of *our* family. Our family is much greater, much larger, and exponentially more amazing than we typically like to think. The evil forces that exist would love nothing more than to disrupt our own earthly families in order to disrupt our spiritual one. We need to fight for our families. But that takes recognizing spiritual activity that could be operating against us. So where does one start?

Something very practical you can do to help discern the spiritual activity operating within your home is to pay attention to family dynamics. Like a car that needs maintenance, it's wise to take time to ensure everything is running smoothly.

Life within the home can be hectic at times. My home consists of five children all under the age of thirteen. My wife and I tend to define the dynamics within our home as organized chaos. There's always so much to do—someone to tend to, somewhere to go, a task that needs to be checked off the to-do list. Everyone is busy and heavily distracted. It's a little bit like the car analogy I mentioned. We become so preoccupied with the destination—getting from one point to another as fast as we can—we often forget to check on the car's condition. We like to put our minds on cruise control and then wait for the check engine light to get our attention. It's at this point that we get a little annoyed, as if the regularly scheduled oil change has invaded our life unexpectedly, when there are other things we'd rather attend to. Stopping life to change the oil is not at the top of our list.

It is the same with our homes. In our desire to get through the day as unscathed as possible, we can fall victim to being surprised when the check engine light of disruption rears its ugly head. But I believe there are some "checks" of our own that we can conduct to make sure things are running smoothly. And we should do them often—every day, in fact.

Take a step back and ask yourself, *is there a sense of rebellion in the air?* If you're married, is your wife submitting to you as Eve did to Adam? Or is your husband neglecting his duties within the home or falling short in loving you? Are you finding yourselves in a cycle of arguing over the most random and nonsensical things? Have you and your spouse neglected the marriage bed (which will absolutely give a foothold to Satan in your home, see 1 Corinthians

7:5)? If you have children, evil spiritual activity could mean they are no longer committing the occasional sin but have now moved into a consistent mode of operating in rebellion. It can seem as if no amount of discipline, conversation, or prayer is changing anything. Examine yourself. Are you avoiding God and what He is commanding of you? Is there a sin that you are apathetic towards and have you begun abusing grace? Has your prayer life tanked along with studying God's Word? Our goal shouldn't be perfection but rather alignment to build God's kingdom in every way. I believe these are very practical things we can do to war against not only our own sinful nature but also against ungodly spiritual activity that could be operating in our homes.

There's almost an art to all of this. On the surface we often chalk up these concerns to just blatant sin. Or, if you're married, to *getting on each other's nerves*. I agree these are sinful behaviors. But when you notice that many of these behaviors are all in operation at the same time, that's a cause for concern. The dynamic of the home will be off. God's kingdom is no longer the focal point. And anyone in the home could be under demonic assault for the purposes of undermining and destroying the family. This is when a fighting married couple need to put their differences aside, love each other no matter what, come together, and pray for the sake of the family. If you're not married, you must meet God and fervently pray for the sake of yourself. For married couples, you must be willing to do whatever is necessary to keep the union intact. If that means also seeking biblical counseling, then do it! Realize, when looking for spiritual activity, you're not looking for drops of rain. You're looking for a storm. So it's important to be able to discern the true work of ungodly spiritual activity from everyday human fallen-ness.

I'd be remiss not to mention the struggles of children here. My childhood was horrible. I couldn't hit the gas pedal fast enough to get myself out of the hell I was experiencing. I learned as a child that parents are easily fooled by the supernatural, and I understand why. As adults we've "wised up" to the foolishness of childhood. We're intelligent, successful, and like to believe we've figured everything out. We become arrogant and prideful. We don't have time for silly superstitions, despite believing a man died, rose from the grave, and then ascended into the clouds. But trust me when I say, *if your child comes to you about monsters in their closet, pray!* Demons don't choose to operate based on what we believe. Parents don't have to believe in demons for them to exist. So pray, even if you don't believe what your child is communicating to you. What's the worst thing that can happen? God intervenes and protects your child? I say it's wise to cover your bases.

Children need to know monsters are real. Where we often fail as parents is we either write off their concerns as overactive imaginations or we do a poor job explaining the true nature of monsters. But just as they need to know monsters are real, they also need to know God is bigger and more powerful than any monster. They need to know they can pray for God's strength. They need to know God is aware and nothing gets by Him.

I am certain there are children all over the world who are being tormented by supernatural evil at this very second. Children are like wide-open playgrounds for demons. Who is going to believe a child who talks about monsters?

Dreams

When God created me, He clearly wasn't concerned about my sleep health. If it wasn't bad enough that my early childhood was plagued with horrors while awake, to this very day I get the pleasure of also dreaming of horrors.

I've always been a vivid dreamer, possessing the ability to manipulate my dreams. As a child I learned a technique in which I could place myself back into a dream that I liked. It was also during my childhood that I learned how to lucid dream. But despite these positives, being a vivid dreamer came with major downsides. I often have nightmares. The slightest things can trigger them. Eating late, not getting enough sleep, getting too much sleep, my sleep paralysis, anxiety, and a host of other things—except, oddly enough, watching scary movies. Nightmares are something I've grown accustomed to.

However, there's another level to my bad dreams. While some dreams I believe are God sent—and these are a rarity—there are others that seem like they've been sent from the pit of hell.

I'm not talking about your normal nightmares of being chased by something or someone. I'm talking about dreams that are so vivid and so disturbing they can only be demonic. Dreams where you're standing in front of a mirror gagging while pulling vines of food from your stomach. Or dreams where you're walking with your friends and one of them is also dragging your dead body. When you arrive at your destination you then have to fold up your own dead body and place it in a trash bag. Yes, there are levels to this, and those aren't the worst of them.

Remember when I mentioned that your calling can attract demonic activity? Don't think just because you're asleep your mind can't be influenced or assaulted. The goal of these dreams is to leave you with anxiety when you wake, to shake you up a bit, to make you miserable due to their disturbed nature, to get you to lose focus. And that's only half of it. If you're getting assaulted while asleep, you're most likely contending with spiritual activity while awake. However, you'll probably be too fatigued to realize where the assault is coming from. All of this will create physical effects on your mind, spirit, and body. Pray, pray, pray! You will have to double down on prayer and hyper-focus on the things of God.

People often like to talk about the grandiose visions and Daniel-like dreams they receive from God. Oh, how many don't realize the demonic plays in that same arena.

Mental Illness

We live in a time when people take mental illness very seriously. I believe this is a good thing. It's been stigmatized for far too long. As someone who once suffered from mental illness—as might be expected after dealing with demons—I know something about this topic. I'm not a certified mental health expert, I don't even pretend to be one, but I know that it is entirely possible for mental illness to be caused by a demonic attack.

In our day the very mention of demon attacks in public will get you shamed, booed, and hissed. What an advantage the demons have. Scripture is replete with demonic possession but even as believers we wouldn't dare suggest someone's mental illness is caused by demonic activity, which is not necessarily the same as demonic possession. We assume that because as believers we can't be possessed—which we can't—then we must be immune to external demonic activity or influence. This is patently false. Jesus was God and Satan showed up to tempt Him. Peter walked with Jesus and Satan still influenced him, causing Jesus to rebuke him.

If you're a believer, you very well could be exposed to demonic forces, and the physical manifestation of the assault could be illness. Remember Job? And sometimes this is *mental* illness.

This doesn't mean *possession*—as believers cannot be possessed (see 2 Corinthians 6:15-16, Colossians 1:13). There isn't a single instance in Scripture where a demon invades a believer. While I can't and wouldn't say someone's mental illness is a direct result of some sort of demonic oppression in a believer's life, I will say it certainly can't hurt to pray for healing. Our God is stronger than any mental illness, and He doesn't discriminate against the brain. Our bodies belong to God. There isn't a single aspect of our nature that God doesn't care about. Just as we can pray for cancer to be healed, we should also be praying for mental illness to be healed. While our scientific and medical advancements are great wonders of the world, we shouldn't idolize our works or presume they should take the place of God.

Now, I do want to be clear as this is a very heavy topic. I absolutely agree there are many variables that can make up someone's mental illness. I'm only advocating that we don't leave God out of our collection of solutions. He should be first. And we shouldn't assume something spiritual can't be at work.

Possession, however, is clearly an entirely different concern and manifests itself in more obvious ways. This is an area that I'm not qualified to speak on at any length. But I will repeat that possession is not something that happens to believers. This is a very challenging subject because severe mental illness can look like possession and vice versa. And before you write this concern off as nonsense, realize there are many Christian board-certified psychiatrists, such as Dr. Richard Gallagher, who diagnose mental illness *and* demonic possession. That's right, science can actually work together with faith, and there is absolutely no reason why they shouldn't.

Laws

Demons operate within positions of power. Remember Ephesians 6:12. Remember the Prince of Persia. Think scale. Think government. Think power.

Some of the easier demonic assaults we can detect are those that operate at scale and ones that seem to take a direct shot at God's moral commandments. Take abstaining from sexual perversion and fornication, for example. The prohibition against these acts is encapsulated within the seventh commandment to not commit adultery. I'll explain.

The people of ancient Israel were forbidden by God from having sex outside of marriage (see Deuteronomy 22:13-30). Israel could not afford to have disease and fatherless children running rampant and a woman was always considered to belong to someone. In ancient Israel women belonged to their father until they married. They then married and belonged to their husband just as husbands belonged to their wives. Sex outside of the marriage bed was considered breaking God's law. If a man was found to have had sex with a single woman, he was to marry her. This was done to protect women and to ensure children had fathers in their lives, unlike today. Remember, Jesus proclaimed that even to look at a woman lustfully was to commit adultery (Matthew 5:28). So clearly adultery doesn't just mean cheating on your spouse. Sex outside of marriage is also adultery because neither man nor woman has been brought together in union under God's sacred act of marriage. Neither belongs to each other. In fact, early in my Christian walk, I was told that until you're married, you belong to your parents. And upon adulthood, you then belong to God. Either way, you don't have sexual rights to another person until marriage. The acts of adultery and fornication are inextricably linked.

When God created Eve, it was done with the purpose of unifying Adam and Eve together. They weren't living in singleness and fornicating. God created a woman for Adam to be with and to help Adam. They were *one* flesh, purposed to operate as a single unit to steward creation.

In our day and age fornication is celebrated throughout the globe and not only by nonbelievers. Apathy towards fornication permeated the church many years ago. I want to be careful here. I don't want to give the impression that the church is some organization apart from the body of Christ. When I say the church has been apathetic, I am talking about *believers*. I've known Christians to encourage their children to fornicate by buying them protection. This is used as a tactic to keep them from experimenting in secret and to ensure they don't have children outside of wedlock. Basically, tossing up their hands, the parents convince themselves it's better for them to shepherd in this sin instead of the world getting to them first. As if there is any difference.

But it doesn't stop there. Pornography became rampant as soon as broadband replaced dial-up modems. Sure, porn preceded broadband, but it wasn't widespread and easy to access. Pornography helped usher in higher divorce rates as it worked to destroy lives and marriages. Riding alongside this train was the gay rights movement, which in America dates back to 1924 with the founding of the Human Rights Society by Henry Gerber. Eventually, America's Supreme Court legalized same-sex marriages in 2015. The legalization and normalization of same-sex marriages continues to make its way all over the world.

And yet the sexual perversion didn't stop there, as many of us knew it wouldn't. The assault on gender started shortly after same-sex marriage was made legal. Public schools are receiving materials to teach children about transgenderism. In 2016 the gender unicorn—a fictional cartoon character—was introduced into the Charlotte-Mecklenburg Schools in North Carolina to train and educate students on transgenderism. What really made this so atrociously wicked was parents had no idea this training was being delivered by the school until after the program began.

With sex being the new god of this age, I have to point out probably the greatest spiritually demonic assault on humanity, which is abortion. God tells us we should not commit murder. So, of course, we commit murder. In fact, the United States—like many other countries in the world—decided to legalize it as a way to further solidify our rebellion against God.

In 1973 the U.S. Supreme Court ruled that individual state laws banning abortion were unconstitutional. This decision was a result of the court case *Roe v. Wade*. A pregnant woman named Norma McCorvey was the plaintiff. Most people don't realize Norma was the victim of a feminist agenda. She was led by two feminist attorneys—Linda Coffee and Sarah Weddington—who were seeking a young naïve woman whom they could use to challenge the abortion law in Texas.

Norma wasn't looking to start a movement and was really used as a pawn by Linda and Sarah. Norma never actually testified in court, was never presented in court, never attended a hearing, and never even read the initial affidavit she was given. In fact, she found out about the landmark decision by reading the newspaper like everyone else in the country.

If this isn't interesting enough, Norma *never* even had the abortion. She gave birth and put her child up for *adoption*. She was also living as a lesbian at the time, but years later turned from that lifestyle. She later led a pro-life group called Operation Rescue to save babies from abortion. In 2003 she even went to court in an attempt to overturn *Roe v. Wade*, but her case was dismissed by the Fifth Circuit Court of Appeals.

But of course, most people don't know the full story because the media did everything it could to silence Norma after *Roe v. Wade*. However, the antics didn't stop there. Over the years it became more difficult to silence Norma, so her angry opponents took things a step further and went to the media with a new story. This story was that Norma was simply a disheveled mess by the time she wandered into the attorney's office desperate to abort her baby. So desperate that she was willing to file a lawsuit. This new story—released in 2017 by *Vanity Fair*[3] —was an attempt to reverse the tide and instead paint attorney Linda Coffee as the heroine.

If you thought the rewriting of history was complete by those who encourage the murder of children, remember Norma was still alive. The problem was that as long as she was alive there was a chance of the lies being corrected or her position being clarified. To combat this, a new story was created and published by the *Los Angeles Times* *after* she died in 2018. This new tale spun by a den of demons was spouted in a selectively edited documentary by FX. They claimed Norma was secretly pro-abortion but had been simply playing the pro-life community for money, which, if I can be frank, is one of the dumbest ideas I've heard in quite some time. Yet people within the

---

3. Joshua Prager, "Exclusive: Roe v. Wade's Secret Heroine Tells Her Story," Vanity Fair, January 19, 2017, https://www.vanityfair.com/news/2017/01/roe-v-wades-secret-heroine-tells-her-story.

pro-abortion camp press their brains to the limit in order to believe it.[4]

Let's use our God-given brains for just a bit. Abortion is a multi-billion-dollar industry. Planned Parenthood alone reported $1.6 billion in income and over $2.0 billion in net assets in its 2019-2020 annual report.[5] If we think about this logically, there was more of an opportunity for Norma to make a far greater amount of money by being the face of the abortion industry. To parade around in secret as an anti-abortionist—a belief you reject—for pennies on the dollar is simply nothing short of lunacy. Yet, people believe this lie because it furthers the agenda of painting Norma McCorvey as one who supported abortion all along.

In America alone millions of babies are murdered every year. This makes the Canaanites look like amateurs.

Everything about *Roe v. Wade* just reeks of demonic activity. Coupled with sexual perversion, abortion is a large-scale assault on a society's moral well-being. Other examples of societal degradation include the Holocaust, the Transatlantic Slave Trade, the Rwandan

---

4. Meredith Blake, "The woman behind 'Roe vs. Wade' didn't change her mind on abortion. She was paid," Los Angeles Times, May 19, 2020, https://www.latimes.com/entertainment-arts/tv/story/2020-05-19/roe-v-wade-jane-roe-norma-mccorvey-hulu-doc-abortion.

5. Prager, "Exclusive: Roe v. Wade's Secret Heroine Tells Her Story."

Genocide, and the atrocities committed by Stalin, Pol Pot, and Mao Zedong.

Large, sweeping changes to a society that run counter to the moral character of God is a good indicator of demonic activity. This doesn't absolve people from being accountable for their sin, but it can explain how such egregious sins can be condoned by a country's governing authority. In fact, the story that ran in the *Los Angeles Times* was released in May of 2020. The timing is significant.

In 2020 America was going through an election season. We were nearing the end of President Donald J. Trump's first term in office. Abortion—skillfully renamed as the Women's Rights Movement—was a big campaign topic of the president's opponents. The Democrats ran hard on the abortion platform, the woman's right to choose to kill her unborn children. President Trump was and is against the murdering of children and therefore was labeled as being against women's rights. The inability to think critically instead of emotionally led many people to fall for this game of word salad.

My point isn't to make a political stand but to encourage you to exercise proper discernment in order to see how *everything* operates together towards a common goal. It's easy to see what is precisely in operation when you take notice of your own government's desires and policies. Pay attention to large sweeping changes. Don't fall victim to the minutiae. War is a long game of strategy. It is a marathon not a sprint.

The Church

Perhaps you've noticed the wave of "spiritual" Christians who have no need for a local church body. Perhaps you've noticed the ever-mounting criticism of the church and of pastors by Christians. Maybe you've witnessed a lack of respect for elder authority. Maybe you've noticed the ethnic division. Maybe you've witnessed the chase for intellectualism while sanctification is no longer a worthwhile goal for some believers.

I have certainly noticed these changes in my own country. I find I'm surprised when I meet believers who actually attend a local church or who serve in some capacity with their time or money. In my experience it's a rarity these days. Hopefully your experience is different. It seems we live in an era of rogue Christianity. Christians who don't realize the importance of 1 Peter 5:8 think they can fare well as solo artists. They are quick to deconstruct their faith in public and then reconstruct it in a vacuum.

Before you say, "no, not my church." Or if you think I'm talking about isolated incidents, I implore you to look up the latest statistics on church defection rates which have been increasing every year.

I firmly believe the demonic realm is eating the church inside and out. The demonic beings in this realm, who have caused so much havoc outside the church, are now wreaking havoc inside the church, at least in America, which has been geeked up on Starbucks, concert-style worship, theological buffets, hangout groups, and preaching that is absent any real conviction. God forbid people ever get offended by the Word of God. We'll preach a sermon on the need for Jesus, justice, or being on mission. But we won't even think about preaching on homosexuality, divorce, adultery, or abortion. No, we reserve those for *special classes* believers must sign up for.

While I believe the church in America is in major trouble, I also can't help but notice the lack of courage and willingness of believers to defend the church. It's so easy to tear it down. It's so easy to criticize every message, every motive, and every decision. It is so easy to flee from the hard work that we're all called to do, like the disciples who abandoned Jesus.

We're more concerned with being accepted by the world—and other believers—than telling the world God will accept them if they'd repent and follow Jesus. This is the demonic influence that has seeped into the church. Our courage has left us. In countries where we have so much, we're scared to lose even a little. But, in lands where persecution is rampant, believers who have little are willing to lose it all.

In America, Christianity has become a lazy affair. So many believers are willing to invest their time, money, and energy in the world. They feed the beast. Every. Single. Day. But not the church. The beautiful body of Christ is not worth *any* investment. We give the world our gold bars and submit pennies to the church. And we often clutch our pearls when called out on it. We lambast the church to justify our lack of giving or commitment. We ignore the persecution of our brothers and sisters around the globe, while still praying that God would somehow bless them, not realizing we're the blessing they need. We've convinced ourselves our part is done because we decided to wear our Jesus apparel to the workplace.

Satan and the entire demonic realm are rendering the church obsolete. Not because the message of the gospel isn't true. Not because Jesus didn't rise from the grave. Not because God has abandoned us. But because we've failed to defend the church with truth and honor. We've failed to chase after God's glory. In this war the church hasn't even shown up for battle. But that hasn't stopped the demonic realm from delivering deafening blows to its body. *Where are the fighters? Where have all the soldiers gone? What are we really willing to lose for the cause of Christ?* Many of us will say our lives, *yes, Lord, our lives!* But in reality we aren't even ready to lose our jobs, our platforms, or our friends.

We must find a way to fight back. We must get to a place where we recognize that the church is bigger than any individual. We must begin to care. We must get over ourselves and our desires. We must begin to truly love the church with all of its blemishes. Because the world will always be more glorifying to God with a blemished church in it than no church at all.

Chapter Ten

Still His Will Not Mine

WELL, HERE WE ARE. Ten chapters in. When we first started on this journey together, I expressed my anguish over God allowing me to endure much agony. Why would God put me through so much pain and suffering? As a child, every fiber of my being was stretched in different directions, tearing at the very foundation of my existence.

When you're experiencing things that are near impossible to put into words, it's equally impossible to react as a normal human being. For example, why didn't I break into my parents' room every night and beg them to oust the monsters that were torturing me? Or why didn't I demand to be taken to the doctor for my nighttime sickness? Why didn't I confide in some other adult and plead for help? The answer to these sorts of questions is quite simple: because I didn't know what to make of anything. I was a child. And, as a child, you're completely out of your league, outmatched, and outfoxed. Nobody believes children when they talk of ghosts and monsters.

For starters, my sicknesses were so far apart—roughly thirty days—it would've been impossible for any doctor, let alone my mother, to determine any real issue. *Was I really sick?*

And what parent truly believes monsters hide in closets? Whenever I mentioned it, I got nothing more than a shrug or laughter. *Silly boy! It's your imagination. Or maybe it is the devil because you've been bad.*

Who do you tell when reality starts to warp in on itself? The incredible nature of spiritual warfare is mind-bending. There's just enough of the spiritual weaving into our world to reveal glimpses of another reality. At the same time, there's only just enough to cause you to doubt your senses. *Am I experiencing something real or is it my imagination? How much evidence do I have to prove my case? Am I really just going crazy? Who believes children anyway?* Certainly not adults, who—in all of their intellectualism—have rationalized all hints of true supernatural activity away and confined it to the depths of the minds of mental patients ... or children.

Today—even as an adult—despite what I know and what I've witnessed, I still wrestle with my childhood horrors. Half of me wants not to believe, while the other half won't allow such a ridiculous thought. There's simply too much evidence. And what should I do with all of this ... evidence? Who would *you* tell? Your average local church pastor will nod and agree, but you'll pick up on the disbelief in their face. I know, as I've seen this doubt piercing through raised eyebrows deceitfully masquerading as belief. Such responses typically come from more conservative Christian circles, from those willing to admit evil exists, but only in some ethereal fashion or only back in the days of Jesus. On the other side you have those who are less conservative and believe far too much about the supernatural world. They don't help either because, to them,

Satan is in the middle of everything. One who is more charismatic makes you feel a bit like you're being mocked or that your experience isn't really a big deal because, hey, *Satan is after everyone and that just means we all have important callings on our lives.* I'm sorry but no, no, no! Satan is absolutely *not* after everyone in the church, and no, everyone does not have some special calling on their lives. And no, you can't claim to believe in supernatural evil and then patronize those who really experience it because your conservative candy-box-of-traditional-theology can't flex enough to make room for the real horrors of this world. The church has much work to do in this area. I'd wager many people are suffering silently from demonic supernatural activity, simply too afraid to speak out on such a taboo topic.

My Father's will be done, not mine. This was the extremely tough lesson I had to learn. Back then, I had no idea that God was preparing and essentially grooming me for His purposes. Oftentimes we call such purposes *ministry*. However, I struggle with this word because it carries baggage and certain ideas. Mention ministry and the mind floods with images of churches, pastors, pulpits, and preaching. To be honest, I've never had much of a desire for any such position. I've only had the desire for people to know the complete picture behind what we think is reality—to know that our eyes and ears are only picking up half of the picture; to know who our Creator is and what's at stake concerning the human race.

While suffering is a difficult pill to swallow—and many of us suffer in different ways—I've been blessed to know there's truly more to life than what my five senses can perceive. Throughout much of my life I believed God hated me and that He failed to protect me. But with age comes wisdom, and I learned that God was actually enabling me to suffer through and protecting me with His strength. He was with me the entire time, knowing that I could handle the trial.

I'm reminded of God's words to Isaiah during Israel's time of needed comfort: "Fear not, for I am with you; be not dismayed, for I am your God; I will strengthen you, I will help you, I will uphold you with my righteous right hand" (Isaiah 41:10).

It's easy to believe God has forsaken us when we experience severe trials. Perhaps it's our guilty conscience from sinful behavior that accuses us daily. When we endure suffering, a knee-jerk reaction is to assume we've done something wrong or somehow have deserved it. But what could we say about Job—a righteous man? Did Job deserve his suffering? Certainly not! Did Jesus? Again, certainly not! For those who seek and love God, we should be slow to assume God is punishing us and quick to remind ourselves that trials do come. And it is under the pressures of these trials that we witness the strength of our Lord. When our God protects, He also builds. He is not in the business of removing all obstacles, which would render us weak and useless.

I praise God for the trial I endured. Don't get me wrong. I hated every millisecond of it. I wouldn't wish it on *anyone*. And there's no amount of money you could pay me to revisit just one day of that childhood experience. But I am glad my God sustained me through it and allowed me to see past the veil that most people will never get to lay their eyes on. To be honest with you, if I had not experienced what I did, I'm not sure I would believe in the supernatural today. Perhaps I would be like many Christians, *believing in the possibility* of demonic supernatural activity but not believing it is real and present.

Hope

So much of what I've shared with you has been heavy, dark, and unrelenting, just like the forces that oppose the body of Christ. But what can get lost in the proverbial shuffle is the message of hope. Christian, we are not alone.

God always had a plan. He was not the least bit surprised when His creation decided to rebel. He is no more surprised than any parent who is shepherding their rebellious children. As a parent I expect my children to rebel. Why? Because I love them. That's right. Children rebel because of our *love for them*.

At the core of love is the willingness to allow others *not* to love you back. God gives His created beings free will. As parents this free will is extended to our children. They have a level of autonomy that allows them to obey or disobey parental authority. All humans possess autonomy which also allows us to disobey God's authority. God—being the perfect Father—will never force anyone to love Him. The moment He decided to give His creation free will, He knew the fall was imminent.

But God, in His infinite wisdom, had a plan for the moral failure humans would endure. When the world's corruption reached what looked like a point of no return, He brought about a flood to cleanse the earth to reestablish order. When Abraham entered the scene, God reached out to enact a covenant with him which eventually led to the formation of Israel. This covenant resulted in the coming of Jesus, which was nothing short of a spiritual rescue mission. Our Lord then confronted Satan and the entire demonic realm to their face in a bold move to reclaim humanity with His blood as payment. Our Lord and Savior then ascended with a promise to return and defeat all who oppose the kingdom of God as well as judge those who reject Him as Lord.

This tells us that God has been fighting for humanity from the very beginning. It tells us that God is not only aware of the spiritual war at play, but He's also actively involved. And while some may argue God caused this war, they couldn't be more wrong. The cause sits squarely at the feet of every creature, whether supernatural or natural, that has decided to use their free agency to reject the Creator.

As Christians we serve a God that is unfathomable—and I mean that in the most amazing aspects of the word. Here is God, the Creator of the universe, who, out of love, perfectly handcrafted beings that could bear witness to His glory. This God—our God—blew existence into reality so all could enjoy Him forever—so our lungs could share His breath. There He was—in the beginning—needing nothing and no one and yet He chose to bring us into *His* world to know Him. Out of love He gave us freedom to turn from Him and we did.

My desire is for you to fully realize the magnitude of this event. Our Creator is not only all-powerful but also all-knowing.

Could you or I, *would* you or I, create such a universe, knowing beforehand that your creation would turn from you? How many of us would assemble a masterpiece for our children knowing they would willingly corrupt it? God, *our amazing God*, knew we would fall and He would have to catch us. God, the one and only true God, predicted we would hate Him. Our God—merciful and gracious in all His ways—knew He would be required to visit us to carry every burden we would ever endure. This God, so rich in love, wrote Himself into a story that placed Himself on the cross after enduring the worst affliction man could exercise upon His flesh. This God, the *only* God, died for His creation. None of this was a surprise. Every moment in time was fully predicted and methodically calculated by the Creator of the universe. Every star was accounted for, every atom was ordered, every grain of sand was personally sifted by our God so we could be in relationship with Him.

When you think about all God is, it is difficult to imagine why anyone would reject Him. Warring against God is a hard thing to grasp. Yet we live in a world filled with demonic forces that know their fate is sealed and their only recourse is to take humanity with them. They are thinking maybe, just maybe, if enough humans are tossed into hell, God would relent and all—even the transgressions of the demons and fallen sons of God—will be forgiven!

For the demonic realm, every day is an opportunity to manipulate and deceive a soul away from God. But our God is not a God of apathy. On the cross He gave His own life to reconcile us back to Him because He cared. On the cross, between gasps of air, He displayed strength that the universe has never seen before. With each drop of blood spilled, my name and your name were being cleansed. As Christ hung on the cross, He looked down at His beloved creation, a mission nearing its end. A mission that started the moment He uttered the most powerful phrase in all existence, "Let there be light."

We are not alone. From our almighty God to heaven's hosts of honor-bound angels, cherubs, and more, there is an army fighting for us and with us. We do not have to fear or lose hope. Never lose hope, Christian. Our God is a God of hope. The empty cross is a symbol of hope. The empty tomb is a symbol of hope. The fulfilled prophecy was a statement of hope written by the fiercest warrior in the entire universe, our God and our Savior, Christ Jesus, our Lord. When He returns His robe will be dipped in blood to lay waste to every evil force that has scorched the earth. And He *will* return.

The battles rage on. Your mission, my mission, *our* mission, is nearing its end. So be the light you are called to be. Be the salt in the earth our Lord knows you to be.

Be hope for a world that *so* desperately needs it. *Move your cross.*

Chapter Eleven

Whom We Love

Our Father, who is in heaven, your power reigns supreme.

There is no foe too formidable for you. There is no army that can overthrow your kingdom.

Your enemies will inhale their own death and destruction.

It is your name that will remain great.

All is brought low before you, Lord of all hosts.

In your hands do heaven and earth rest.

The balance of all things belongs to you.

By your strength we are made strong.

With your Word, we pierce the veil of darkness.

Your command is our battle cry, and we will sing your praises until death, for you have given us life and a will to live.

No stronghold can resist your might.

There is no other glory. None but yours, O God.

There is no other God but you, O Lord.

And for you whom we love we will fight.

About Author

This is the page where you'd normally expect to find a list of accolades, famed accomplishments or degrees written in the third person. I've always found this practice odd. Surely you already know my name as it's on the cover of the book. And during my lifetime I've learned that the wisdom of man is foolishness to God. I've seen many men weighted down with accolades fall from grace like a flaming meteorite.

I've also learned God changed the world with twelve, very ordinary men. Men without influence, high status, fame or platforms. Ordinary men who desired the wisdom of God so that they may know Him. That is me. I'm an ordinary man, graced by an extraordinary God with a story to tell the world.

However, I'd be remiss to not mention my better half and help mate-my wife-who has blessed me with her companionship and five children. She's my support beam that enables me to do God's work.

You can contact me at www.terrencecovin.com